Alex Russell

The Fundamentals of Printed Textile Design

ethical: aware-
ness/
reflect-
ion/
debate

ava
academia

Table of Contents

 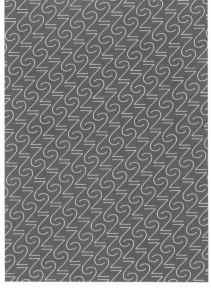 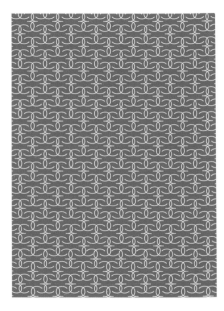

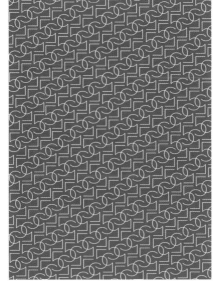

Introduction

This book is about contemporary practice in printed textile design. It provides an introduction to the creative skills, techniques and processes required by designers in order to produce a professional, creative and commercially aware portfolio. In order to design effectively, print and pattern practitioners need to understand not only how the industry works but should ideally also be aware of, for example, the cultural and economic factors that can shape what future clients or consumers will require. The book suggests strategies for developing an understanding of these contexts within and beyond the fashion and textiles industry. It explores the key elements of the subject to provide an innovative resource for the designers of today and tomorrow.

Trying to describe what printed textile designers do is not quite as straightforward as it might at first appear. Taken at face value, printed textile design is the creation of imagery or pattern to be applied to cloth. In fact, the definition is slightly misleading, as its practitioners may also design for other surfaces such as wallpaper, gift-wrap or any other product which may be printed on or embellished. They may describe themselves as surface pattern designers or graphic designers for fashion; even if the word 'textile' does appear on a business card or within a job description, the role may not involve actually working with fabric on a day-to-day basis.

However, in amongst this tangle are a few key points that unite design practitioners in this field. They are creating decoration or ornament that is applied to a product in order to add to its value in some way. The form and content of their designs are framed to a large degree by both the nature of the product and the printing technology used to embellish it. They are most frequently employed by the fashion, home / interiors or giftware / stationery sectors.

Getting started as a professional designer requires hard work and patience. A major part of this book is devoted to showing what skills are required to break into the business and how best to communicate design talent in order to do so. It aims to present an honest and balanced overview of how the industry works and what it needs from designers.

You may find your own experiences do not reflect some of the content of this book. The design process is not linear or prescriptive; from any given starting point, ten designers would probably come up with ten very different design outcomes about which ten different clients would have very differing opinions. There is no substitute for putting in the hours to get good at the skills or in actively researching how the part of the design world that interests you actually works. The infinite variation out there is part of what makes this such an exciting world to forge a career in. All this book is trying to do is nudge you in the right direction.

Work hard, don't mess with copyright, have fun.

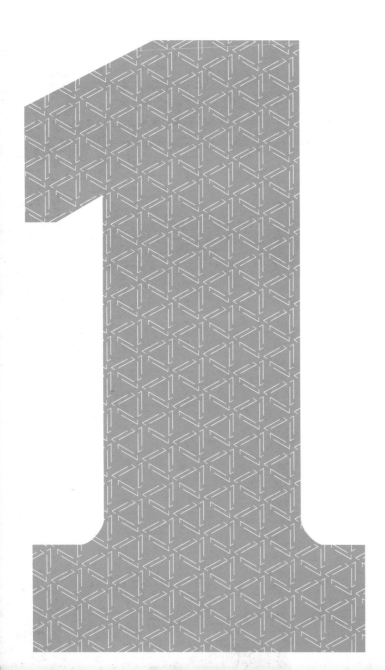

The framework

In order to develop an understanding of contemporary printed textile design, it is important to know about its context. This area of design has a rich history that has a significant influence on current practice. In particular, this affects both the imagery that designers work with and the requirements of the methods by which designs are printed or applied to fabric (or other substrate). This chapter starts with a brief overview of past practice, exploring the multicultural mix of design elements that inform the visual language of print and pattern.

The next step is to look at how the industry works today, exploring how designs are used on products, and the part practitioners play in what may be a lengthy and complex process. This leads into looking at the future of the discipline – how digital technology is likely to affect manufacturing once digital fabric printing becomes more common than rotary screen printing, and other significant factors on the future such as sustainability and ethical issues.

Printed textile design history

Printed textile design has a long history. Images over 4000 years old in Egyptian tombs show patterned clothing and there is evidence that similar fabrics existed in the same period in Eurasia. Whilst it is likely that these would have been hand painted, the use of blocks to stamp pattern onto cloth is believed to date back at least 2000 years in India; similar technology existed in China at the same time, although it is unclear if this was specifically used for printing textiles.

It might be easy to assume that it is only recently that the design and manufacture of printed textiles became a global business, but fabric has actually been a staple of trade routes for centuries. It wasn't until the eighteenth century that European print design came close to matching the quality of pattern from Asia, not least due to the development of copper plate printing. Despite the advances in technology in the West, the influence of Asian design, both in style and in content, formed the bedrock of European design and is clearly visible to this day.

Even the briefest look at printed textile design's past demonstrates two highly significant influences on the practice: Firstly, that a significant proportion of new designs are updated or adapted versions of existing designs, some based on patterns that are thousands of years old. Secondly, that the technology used to print the designs has a profound effect on the practice of creating print and pattern design.

Dyeing techniques
In most printing techniques, the design is applied to the substrate by printing colour onto it. This sounds obvious, but some of the oldest methods of getting pattern onto cloth used a different method. This involves applying the design using either a resist or a mordant.

Resist printing
In the resist method, the textile is painted or printed with some form of substance that acts as a mask when the fabric is subsequently dyed. For example, the Indonesian batik technique involves applying melted wax to the cloth, either by brush, by special pen-like tools called tjantings or by tjaps, stampers generally made of strips of metal. The wax cools almost immediately to form a barrier. When the fabric is (cold water) dyed, all the untreated bits of fabric pick up the colour, but the areas protected by the wax remain as they were. The textile is then boiled, which melts the wax out of it, revealing the design. Different versions of the batik process can be found in Africa, Europe and other parts of Asia.

A number of alternatives to wax can also be used. These include pastes made of rice or other starch-based ingredients and clay. In Nigeria, the Yoruba people create designs on fabric called adires using starch paste. The fabric is hand painted with the paste and then dip dyed in indigo. The cloth may then have additional areas masked out by the starch and be re-dyed. This process gives a range of different blue tones.

'Find beauty not only in the thing itself but in the pattern of the shadows, the light and dark which that thing provides.'

Junichiro Tanizaki

Tie dyeing

Another variation of the resist technique is tie-dying. Thread is used to firmly bind areas of the fabric, sometimes by knotting small objects like seeds into the cloth or by stitching into it and drawing the threads tight, or by tying pleats or other folds. When dyed, the colour cannot get through to the areas (say) wrapped in thread or into the inner folds and the pattern is revealed after rinsing and removing the threads or flattening the fabric out. The process was developed in India (where the technique is called bandhana), Africa (in Zaire, for example) and Japan (the process is known as shiboru). The technique has been used in recent years by a number of fashion designers, including Berhardt Willhelm's Autumn Winter 2008 / 2009 womenswear collection.

Mordant printing

Mordant printing works by the opposite principle to resist printing. A mordant is a chemical that works as a fixing agent, significantly increasing the permanence of the colour of a dyestuff. The pattern is applied to the cloth by painting or printing the mordant on, generally thickened in some way to prevent it bleeding. When the textile is subsequently dyed, the areas with the fixing agent take up the colour much better and appear significantly darker when the cloth is rinsed out. The process was used fairly widely by Indian printers (often applied by block), following the refinement of the process from the sixteenth century onwards.

Resist and mordant printing today

Because resist and mordant printing are time consuming processes, generally involving a lot of work by hand, they are not now widely used in mass production. However, the design styles they generate remain influential and there are specialist printers, particularly working with batik techniques, who do use the process. These include Vlisco, a Dutch company, and the ABC Wax company (based in Manchester, UK) and its sister company Akosombo Textiles Ltd (in Ghana). These companies use copper roller printing techniques to apply the resist to the fabric, almost all of which is sold to the African market.

Block printing

Block printing is a relief technique, meaning that the colour is applied to the raised areas of the printing surface (as opposed to intaglio printing techniques such as copper engraving). Until copper plate and roller printing became common in the West towards the end of the eighteenth century, block printing was the prevalent method of applying pattern to both fabric and wallpaper in much of the world. Although it is currently only really used as a specialist or craft technique, there have been signs of its use increasing recently, probably as a result of increasing concerns about the ethics and sustainability of more common mass production techniques.

A block is made for each colour in the design; if this is very large, a number of blocks may be required for each colour. Blocks are normally made by carving the design out of wood. Very fine lines, too fragile for wood alone, are achieved by inlaying metal strips. Large areas of flat colour are difficult to achieve as the dyestuff will not always coat the wood evenly; to get around this, felt is applied to these areas, giving a much more uniform print. Tiny points of metal called pitch pins are inserted into the corners of each block. These leave a little dot of colour on the printed surface that can be used to position the next print with the same block, or one of another colour.

Above right:
Old printed textiles, often a rich source of inspiration for contemporary designers, are likely in turn to reference pre-existing patterns. This block-printed French design from 1870 draws heavily on Indian traditions.

To print the design, the block is coated with colour by pushing it onto a fine cloth, stretched over a resilient base and liberally brushed with dyestuff. The block is positioned on the fabric or paper using the pitch pins and the design is transferred by holding it steady and hitting the back of it with a special mallet called a maul. The block is then re-coloured and printed in the next place.

Despite some attempts to mechanize the process, block printing was widely replaced with copper roller printing during the nineteenth century, mainly because the latter was so much faster in comparison. Block printing did, however, continue as a technique for high-end markets for some years, notably to print William Morris's wallpaper and chintz designs.

'Just as appetite comes
by eating, so work begins
inspiration, if inspiration is not
discernible at the beginning.'

Igor Stravinsky

AUTHOR TIP
INSPIRATION LIBRARY

One of the most helpful resources a designer can have is a library of images. You should get into the habit of collecting a wide range of source material. Try to be objective about this – look for images that will help you to build up a broad understanding of all different kinds of print and pattern, not just the ones that are your favourites. This should include examples of historical designs from as many different times and cultures as you can find.

You can do this in one of two ways – on paper or online. For the former, files can be more practical than sketchbooks as it's easier to re-order or take individual pages out (to pin up with a range of other images as inspiration for a particular project, for example). For the latter, blogs (such as www.blogger.com or www.wordpress.com) or photo sharing sites (such as www.flickr.com or www.photobucket.com) are free and easy to set up and give an ideal way of cataloguing all the images you collect from the web or from your own photography.

In either case, try to always add a note as to where you found the image and what information you know about it. It's quicker to do this as you go, rather than trying to track it down later.

'It has been said that the Indian subcontinent is the most original, creative and prolific source of patterned textile production in the world.'

Drusilla Cole

Right:
An Indian palampore, showing a tree of life design that proved hugely influential in European printed textile design.

Indian design

In seventeenth-century Europe, the design and manufacture of woven or embroidered designs had achieved very high levels of quality (and price), and prints were often made as cheap copies of them. Around this time, European countries began to trade increasingly with Asia, and hand-painted designs from India, known as calicos or chintzes, became a key element of this commerce. The imagery on these fabrics, often in the form of palampores, was a revelation and made printed fabric, hitherto seen as a cheap imitation of weaving or embroidery, highly covetable in its own right in the West for the first time. As demand for this fabric increased, traders encouraged manufacturers in India to use block printing as well as hand painting to increase production volume. Attempts were made to manufacture similar products in Europe, but these initially lacked the quality of the contemporary Indian textiles, both in design and printing terms. By the 1750s, however, European manufacturers began to acquire most of the design and technical skills to achieve fabrics of comparable quality.

The influence of Indian design

In design terms, the Indian fabrics had an immeasurable effect on practice in Europe. When European manufacturers began to properly train print designers for the first time, the demand was for cloth that looked like it was of Indian origin. The framework for this training was working in the styles of Indian chintzes and calicos; the European designers were essentially taught to design in an Indian style. Of course, in time new styles developed and as trade increased around the world, patterns from a wide range of different cultures were added to the mix. However, many key parts of the language of printed textile design, particularly with regard to florals, can be traced directly back to the skill of Indian designers.

This was an early instance in Europe of a practice that continues to this day – subtly updating existing patterns to sustain the demand for them. It is also worth noting the cyclical nature of the print industry. In the mid-1680s, there was a huge manufacturing base in India for the European market. Less than 100 years later, this had disappeared as the skills became adopted in the West. By the end of the nineteenth century, the UK was printing a vast amount of fabric and exporting it all over the world. One hundred years on, much of the manufacturing base has shifted back to the East.

Copper plate printing

Copper plate printing on cloth is thought to have originated in Ireland in the early eighteenth century. It is an intaglio process; the design is cut into the surface of a copper plate. The plate is covered in dyestuff and the surface wiped clean so that colour remains in the cut lines below the surface. This is then transferred to the fabric with a press. The technique, similar to etching, is particularly suited to highly detailed, line-based imagery.

How printed textile designers worked with this new development shows the influence of new technology on the practice. Designs are frequently of a single colour (engraving the plates is highly laborious and registration of different plates difficult), tend to make extensive use of cross-hatching to achieve shading (the process is well suited to fine delicate lines) and often have areas of detailed pattern in empty space (trying to accurately join the pattern from the bottom of one print to the top of the next was difficult with the large, heavy plates).

The imagery that designers used also trod new ground. The process was very similar to how illustrations of the time would have been printed, and many of the designs have a narrative quality. Decorative painting also proved popular, with bucolic or pastoral scenes common in the work of designers such as Jean-Baptiste Huet, who trained as a painter and was commissioned by Oberkampf to create many of the famous Toiles de Jouy. It is probably worth noting that this is one of the first names in textile design to have been recorded; to this day, most printed textile design is anonymous.

Left:
Toiles de Jouy designs, created at the Oberkampf factory in France, show the influence of the process of copper plate printing on design. The image is single colour, features linear shading and has areas of empty space to allow the repeat to be hidden.

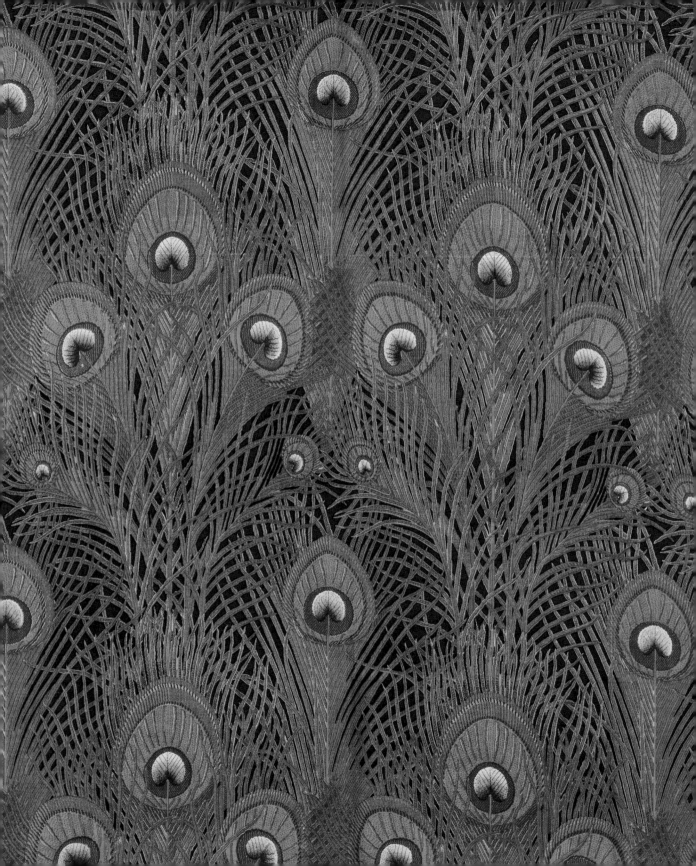

Opposite:
Silver Studios
design by Arthur
Silver for Liberty.

Copper roller printing

By the end of the eighteenth century the process had been adapted to copper roller printing. Instead of flat plates, the designs are cut into the surface of copper tubes. These are then mounted into a machine. This rotates the rollers, covers them in dyestuff, scrapes the surface clean and rolls fabric over it, picking up the colours of the pattern from the cuts. A number of rollers can be mounted in the same machine, allowing a range of colours to be printed at once. Crucially, the process is fast – entire bolts of fabric can be printed without stopping. It took some time to replace block printing, however, mainly because engraving the rollers was a highly skilled and lengthy process. However, the invention of mechanical engraving machines helped it to gain ground, and, with invention of photographic etching providing a further update of the technology in the twentieth century, it was the main method of printing until screen printing became mechanized.

Synthetic dyestuff

In addition to advances in printing technology, there was another development that had a profound effect on textile design practice in the mid-nineteenth century. Up until that time, all dyestuff was directly derived from naturally occurring sources. Many colours were only obtainable via complex, closely guarded recipes that might be prohibitively expensive for printers to use. Mass-produced cloth could often not be produced in the spectrum of colour available today.

In 1856, a chemist based in Manchester, UK, called William Perkin, developed a synthetic purple dye from coal-tar. This was followed by a wide range of discoveries across Europe that eventually provided print and pattern designers with a full rainbow to work with. Designs that featured saturated colour quickly became popular; so admired and quickly accepted was Perkin's Purple that accounts of fashion of the time may refer to it as the 'Mauve Decade'.

When William Morris began textile designing in the 1860s, he felt that the synthetic colours were crude and that mechanization had resulted in increasingly poor design standards, with manufacturers focusing on quantity rather than quality. Although his laudable ideas about good design being available for all were at odds with the high cost of his fabrics and wallpapers, his work was highly influential and a number of his designs remain available to this day through Sanderson. Other Arts and Crafts Movement designers such as C.F.A. Voysey and Walter Crane created designs that were influenced by Indian, Chinese and Japanese decorative pattern, and thanks to the skills of designers such as Arthur Silver, companies like Liberty became famous for their printed textiles. It should be noted, however, that there is some evidence that the designs of Morris and other luminaries of the Arts and Crafts Movement were more appreciated by manufacturers on mainland Europe rather than in the UK. Although these designs feature heavily in source books and histories of the practice (and justifiably so), they actually found their way into relatively few homes and interiors.

The emergence of screen printing

In the 1920s, textile design printers began to use a new technique: screen printing. Copper roller printing had become ever easier to convert designs for, but the expensive process of engraving the rollers and setting up the machines was only cost effective when large quantities of fabric were to be printed. High-end fashion in particular needed a way of quickly and comparatively cheaply printing shorter runs of textiles (block printing was also too laborious) and looked to screen printing for the first time.

Screen printing developed from stencilling, a process that has been used all over the world, mainly using paper or very thin metal. It reached particularly high levels of quality in Japan, where it has been used since the eighth century as a method of transferring pattern to fabric.

The flat screen process

In basic screen printing, a mesh of fabric is stretched over a frame. In the areas where the pattern is, the mesh is left open; other areas are blocked with a coating (or stencil). Dyestuff is pushed through the screen with a squeegee (normally a blade of rubber) and goes through the open areas in the mesh, transferring the pattern to the surface underneath.

Although paper stencils can be used to do this, the pattern is normally transferred to the screen by a photographic process. Each colour of the design is transferred to a transparent film, either by hand painting, photography or reprographic methods, so all elements of pattern are opaque. The film is then placed on a screen that has been coated with a light-sensitive emulsion and exposed to light (normally UV), which makes the emulsion become waterproof where it hits it. When the screen is washed, the parts that were opaque on the film, protected from the light, rinse away, leaving a durable design on screen.

Right:
This design by Barbara Brown from the 1960s makes good use of screen printing's ability to print large areas of flat colour.

For the first time, this meant that any image that could be drawn, painted or photographed could be very quickly and easily set up for printing on fabric or other surfaces. This proved particularly popular with high-end fashion companies, who appreciated the new styles that this allowed printed textile designers to develop. The influence of contemporary painting is very evident in a lot of designs from this time.

Right:
A pattern for
rotary screen
printing from the
freelance portfolio
of designer
Claire Roberts.

Screen printing for mass production

Screen printing became mechanized in the 1950s, initially retaining the flat screen that the hand printing process uses. It gradually began to gain ground on copper roller printing. The automated process positions the fabric under the screens, which are then lowered onto it. Squeegees are mechanically drawn over the screen and the screens then lift off the fabric, which is then moved into the next position. Each colour requires a different screen.

As the 1960s progressed, rotary screen printing became more developed, which significantly increased printing speeds – the stop-start positioning of the fabric with flat bed machines is not particularly mechanically efficient. Rotary screens consist of a tube, made of very thin metal such as nickel. Tiny holes are etched or laser cut from the metal in the shape of the pattern. The tubes are supported at either end by more substantial construction and have a fixed squeegee and dyestuff supply inside them. The fabric is run underneath in a not dissimilar way to copper roller printing. As it does so, the holes that make up the design on the rotary screen move under the squeegee, which pushes the colour through them onto the cloth's surface. A number of colours can be printed at once with the addition of subsequent rotary screens. This process eventually superseded roller printing, and is the most common production technique in use today.

Although hand screen printing is still used for some high-end or craft based work, the overwhelming majority of fabric printing is now done by rotary screen. Whilst this is based on the same technology, the complexity of the machines makes it an expensive process to set up for a new design, means they are not suited to printing in small quantities ('short runs'). Digital printing is increasingly used for this instead.

Other printing techniques

There are a few other print processes that are worth noting, even though they may not have been used particularly widely. This is not intended as an exhaustive list, but does include the ones you are most likely to come in contact with.

Transfer printing

The design is printed onto paper first, in most cases with disperse dyestuff. The paper is then heat pressed onto the fabric; the action of the heat vaporizes the dyestuff, transferring into the fabric (hence the name). As disperse dye only works on some fabric (such as polyester), the process does have limitations. It does, however, allow photographic imagery to be printed using half tone or CMYK separations, which is not generally possible with screen printing. Other versions do exist that allow natural fabrics to be printed in this way, often by pre-treating the fabric.

Lithography

Historically, a number of attempts were also made to mechanize the lithography process for use on fabric, but this proved very difficult to register accurately and was only used in isolated instances. The lithography process has long been a mainstay of the paper printing industry, however, and designers working in (say) the giftware or stationery sectors are highly likely to create designs that will be printed by a lithographic process, generally off-set litho.

'The digital revolution is far more significant than the invention of writing or even of printing.'

Douglas Engelbart

Off-set litho

The image to be printed is normally separated into four colours: cyan, magenta, yellow and black (CMYK). Each separation is made up of tiny dots of varying size, which, when printed together, optically mix to give the final image. The dots run at different angles to prevent interference patterns appearing. In some cases, areas of colour (or other finishes such as glosses or metallics) are used in combination with (or instead of) the CMYK separations. These areas are known as spot colours. Although it is not normally referred to as such, screen printing could be thought of as a spot colour process, as each colour is applied individually. (Screen printing is used as a paper printing process, but normally in short runs or limited editions such as fine art prints.) Commercial lithography quickly made use of photography towards the end of the nineteenth century, and made similarly prompt use of digital technology.

Wallpaper printing

This uses a variety of different methods, some of which are fairly exclusive to that end-use. Rubber rollers may be used, giving a particularly irregular texture to the print. Other wallpaper techniques may involve embossing, flocking or altering the surface in other ways. Very high-end wallpaper may be printed by hand - possibly the most labour intensive versions of these are the panoramic scenes created by the Zuber company. Contemporary high-end designs may use digital technology, such as the giclée printed wallpaper commissioned from a range of designers and artists by the Maxalot company.

Ceramic transfer

Surface pattern designers working in the ceramics industry may have their designs transferred onto the product using this method. The design is screen or digitally printed onto special paper using enamel powder and then transferred onto the ceramic.

DISCUSSION POINT
FAKING OLD TECHNOLOGY

The superseding of block printing by copper
plate and roller printing caused a particular
reaction. The small dots of colour that block
printing's pitch pins left on the fabric, actually
an undesired part of the method, became
seen as a mark of quality. In some cases,
little dots were added in strategic places
to designs destined for copper roller printing
to make them look as if they had been block
printed. Think about what parallels could be
drawn with this and the introduction of screen
printing and digital printing.

Printing in the future

Printed textile design's journey to the twenty-first century has been long and global and has seen big technological changes, particularly in the last 250 years. Although contemporary designers in industry are highly unlikely to ever come into direct contact with any of the historical printing processes, it is important to know about them because they have had a huge influence on the way practitioners have worked. The visual language of print and pattern has been shaped by the past to a very large degree; the possibilities of the technologies involved have been central to this. The impact of digital technology, discussed in more detail on pages 30–35, is likely to change the design and production process to a very large degree. Designers who are aware of how clients and customers responded to changes in technology and design process in the past are not only likely to be more equipped to deal with the exciting new possibilities on the horizon, but also better able to convince others of the benefits of change.

Left:
Dan Funderburgh's Chinatown design uses visual language from both traditional Chinese pattern and the pastoral scenes typical of eighteenth-century French companies such as Oberkampf.

Careers in printed textile design

Right:

The Deanne Cheuk design opposite seen on a dress from Sue Stemp's A/W 2007 collection.

There probably isn't such a thing as a typical professional printed textile designer. Practitioners working today may be employed by a single company, may freelance or (increasingly commonly) have a portfolio career that involves working in a range of different ways, often simultaneously. Some print and pattern jobs may be done by (say) graphic designers or illustrators, whilst printed textiles designers may find themselves designing for a whole range of products other than fabric-based ones.

Practitioners essentially are creating commercially viable print or pattern to fulfil the need of a particular client requirement. It is important to understand that the work most printed textile designers do is generally a very small part of a complex production process that involves a large number of other people. It is also necessary to know that how a design looks may change significantly in the time between the designer finishing it and it going into production. Designs may be re-coloured, re-scaled, have elements removed or changed or be used as inspiration by other practitioners rather than on a product.

The function of printed textile designers

Designers answer briefs. The content of a brief may be very vague or conceptual or it may be highly detailed, but in most cases, a practitioner will be given some kind of outcome to design for, and some indication of what imagery and colour to use. The process essentially involves using this information to create print or pattern designs that meet the needs of the client. In turn, these designs are essentially a set of instructions that the client's printer, contractor or manufacturer will use to transform a product, surface or substrate.

The role of printed textile designers

It can be helpful to think of the role of the printed textile designer as supplying a service rather than a product. As a working practitioner, you need to be able to balance a range of technical skills (putting designs into repeat, for example, to understanding how the print process will affect the way colour is used) with the aesthetic decision-making needed to visually answer the brief. This service is one link in a long chain, but one that has a highly significant impact on the final product. In business terms, applying print or pattern to a product is a method of increasing its desirability. In purely functional terms, printing a design onto, say, a furnishing fabric has no effect on its performance – it won't make the sofa cover last any longer or feel any different from one in identical fabric with no print. However, the style that the pattern creates has a major impact on the customer's decision of what to buy and gives the manufacturer the chance to increase both the allure and the profit margin.

Areas of printed textile design

Printed textile designers most commonly create designs for use in the following areas:

Home / interiors

Designs for furnishing fabrics, bedding, curtains, blinds, wallpapers, carpets, rugs or any other surface in any interior space that can have pattern applied to it. Can also include kitchenware / ceramics and similar products and may overlap with giftware.

Fashion

Print and pattern for men's, women's or children's garments, footwear, accessories or any other related product.

Giftware / stationery

Designs for wrapping paper, cards and any stationery that has pattern on it – notebook cover, files and so on.

In addition to creating designs for a wide range of products, printed textile practitioners may work in related areas such as trends or predictions, styling, brand identity and art direction.

Prior to the establishment of design schools, designers would have been apprenticed and learnt their skills via methods including copying existing designs and preparing more senior designers' work for printing (by separating it into its individual colours, for instance). Although many designers do now receive specialist training as part of the working process, particularly early in their careers, most now obtain a degree qualification before embarking on employment.

Above:
Flowers are probably the most common subject matter in print and pattern. This design by Deanne Cheuk mixes peonies and palm trees in a graphic style.

The twenty-first-century design career

Recent years have seen a shift in the way that many people spend their working lives. Many people setting out on a career, particularly in the creative industries, have what is known as portfolio employment – working for relatively short times for individual employers, working on more than one job at a time, or combining freelance work with paid employment. In some cases, particularly early in someone's working life, this may involve a non-creative job that pays the bills while gaining experience through placements or establishing a freelance practice. More experienced designers may have particular clients who provide a regular basic income, giving them scope to get involved with more speculative projects.

Print and pattern in furnishing

In most instances, designers working for home and interior markets create their work in repeat. The scale of the products that they design for (duvet covers, for example) means that practitioners in this field often work to a much larger scale than their fashion counterparts. Some designs may be placements (for blinds, for example, or use on crockery), but the ability to work in repeat is normally obligatory in this area, not a desirable extra.

Although there are many examples of genuine innovation in the sector, trends do tend to be slower moving than in fashion – successful products are more likely to remain in production (as long as they continue to sell), rather than automatically be replaced every six months as they are in the clothing sector.

Print and pattern in fashion

The idea that printed textile designers are supplying a set of instructions that are used by the manufacturer to create the final printed product is particularly apparent in fashion. It is common for designs that are intended to be used as all-overs to merely suggest this, not be in actual, technically accurate repeat. There are signs that this is starting to change – designing digitally makes it much quicker to experiment with repeat; but it remains the case that many designers creating all-overs for fashion don't put them in repeat themselves. A significant number of designs for the fashion sector are not intended to be in repeat at all. Designs are often single motifs or graphics (for t-shirts, for example) or other prints engineered or placed on a specific part of a garment. Practitioners working in this sector are often referred to as graphic designers rather than printed textile designers.

Print and pattern in other areas

Designers creating for giftware, stationery and other areas are in many cases creating print and pattern that will be transferred onto the product by techniques other than screen printing. Much giftwrap, for example, is printed with four-colour separation processes such as offset litho, whereas those designing for tableware are likely to have their designs printed using the ceramic transfer process. The nature of the output varies widely with the product; repeat or placement designs may be required.

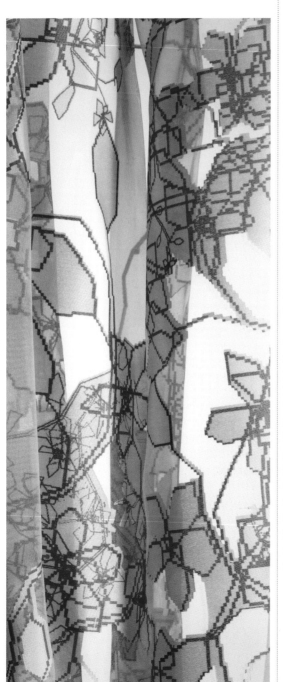

Retail and manufacturing employers

There are any number of routes that a printed textile designer's career may follow, but if they are employed (as opposed to freelance), probably the most typical is working for a company that retails or produces printed or pattern product and has an in-house design studio. This normally involves one or more designers, employed to create print and pattern for use on that company's products or as part of their service. The exact nature of what this entails will vary, but typically practitioners will work to answer briefs, either creating new print designs or adapting existing ones. Larger studios are likely to have some kind of career path from junior to senior designer positions; the latter may involve the authorship of briefs and more responsibility for overall design direction (and lesser amounts of hands-on design work) or be more focused on management.

Retailer in-house studios tend to be more common in larger companies for a number of reasons. In many cases, particularly with fashion, print designs are only required at particular points in the year and the timeframe between the company deciding how the overall collection should look (and hence what the print design brief is) and it going into production is relatively short. For small businesses, this may mean that it is difficult to justify employing a full time designer. Companies that do have in-house designers fairly commonly buy in additional designs from agencies or freelancers. These might not be put into production; the designs might be used as inspiration for the in-house team, or be adapted into two or more separate prints.

Left:
Tord Boontje's designs have featured on a wide variety of different products. This is one of his designs for the Danish company Kvadrat.

Agencies

An agency is a business that sells designers' work to a range of companies. Some focus on a particular market sector, whilst others sell to a broader range of clients. Most agencies sell in more than one country and many sell in several continents. Some agencies are highly structured, with a clear hierarchy and set roles for each employee, with set positions for sales and marketing as well as design. Others operate on a more fluid basis, with (for example), designers creating new work at some times and selling designs at others.

Some agencies employ designers and pay them a set wage, regardless of how many designs each individual designer sells. Other agencies pay their designers a percentage of the amount they sell that designer's work for, typically 55 to 60 per cent of the sale price. Some operate somewhere between the two - the agency pays its designers a retainer (a set monthly or weekly amount), which is then deducted from their sales. A few agencies charge significantly less commission, but charge their designers a set fee for showing work to clients.

Broadly speaking, agencies sell in up to three ways. The first involves showing their collections directly to potential clients. The agency will set up appointments, normally visiting a selection of clients in the same area around the same time. The second is via trade fairs. Agencies rent space, normally charged by the square metre, and clients visit the fair in order to buy designs. The final method involves a client commissioning designs, rather than buying them from the portfolio. They present the agency with a brief of some sort, which it then gives to its design team to work on. In addition to supplying designs, agencies may also offer other services.

Some agencies have their own studio space for their design team. This tends to be more common with agencies who employ their designers, rather than those using freelance practitioners, but there are a number of studios who do operate with the latter method. The role that the designers play may be the straightforward creation of print and pattern, but others may work on tasks such as the printing of fabric (if the agency present their work via fabric samples or blanks) or colourway work.

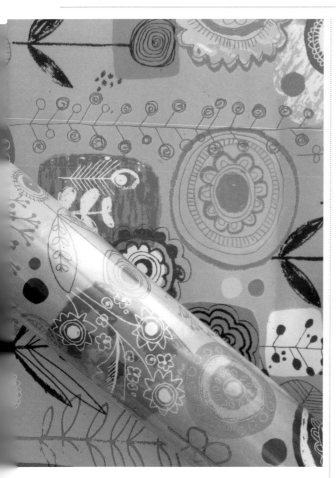

If this is the case, it's common that agencies sell to different markets or in different geographic regions. Other designers work directly with clients, rather than via an agency – in most cases these are practitioners with sufficient experience to have built up the contacts to do this. It is likely that they will operate in a similar way to an agency, by making appointments directly with potential clients and exhibiting at trade fairs. Some freelancers combine working with agencies and working directly with clients, or with salaried work.

Freelancers generally work from home or a rented studio space, although some work on their agency premises. Although they do essentially work as part of a team (answering client or agency briefs), their working day can be quite isolated and those designers who work outside the home may share studio space or premises with other people working in the creative industries.

Left:
Paperchase use a wide range of print and pattern designers for their giftware and stationery.

Freelance designers

Freelancers earn a living by selling designs or related services to clients either directly or via an agency (or both). They only receive money for what they sell (rather than earning a monthly wage, say) and are generally responsible for keeping their own accounts and sorting out their own taxes (or paying an accountant to do this). Some freelancers work exclusively with one agency, but others may have two or more.

Printed textiles and digital technology

Right:

Basso and Brooke make full use of the possibilities of digital fabric printing in their textile designs.

Digital technology has already had a huge impact on printed textile design. Most job specifications expressly mention software skills as an essential requirement and the design process is increasingly computer-based. Although the adoption of the technology has been slower than in some other areas of design, a software skills base is absolutely crucial for future designers.

It is important to appreciate that the technology can be used to create designs in any style, even ones that appear very old. Equally, working by hand and working digitally are not mutually exclusive. It may be that designers work with scans of paintings or drawings, assembling the repeat with software. Even if designs are entirely hand painted, the print process is highly likely to involve digitization of some form.

The emergence of digital design

In contrast to other areas of the creative industries such as graphics or product design, print and pattern design was fairly slow in the up-take of digital technology. The reasons for this were manyfold, but analogue manufacturing processes and the perception that a hand-painted design was more likely to be unique were probably at the heart of this. Textile designers have been increasingly working with digital media since the mid-1990s. It is rare to see any kind of job description that doesn't mention one or more types of software by name and whilst traditional drawing and painting media may play a part in the design process, final designs are ever-increasingly in digital format, particularly when produced in-house.

Designing with digital media

Initially, the software that printed textile designers used was quite commonly specialist software that essentially translated the traditional methods of creating patterns or other designs into the digital arena. Functions had names that designers would be acquainted with and did things on screen they'd been doing with paint and paper. These early systems (and the hardware required to run them) were generally very expensive (prohibitively so for most freelance designers) and often complex to operate.

Although the specialist software is still used by some companies, in recent years an ever-increasing number of designers have gravitated towards Adobe® software, initially using Photoshop® and subsequently Illustrator®. Whilst this software's tools are more likely to have been derived from graphics or photography techniques, the programs offer a sufficiently broad range of possibilities to allow textile designers to create designs using a standard platform, reinforced by the ubiquity of Creative Suite® software in both education and industry.

Whilst styles and printing technologies have changed, the methods used by practitioners to physically create designs had, until recently, changed very little in a long time. The processes visible in surviving design sketches from as long as 200 years ago don't look wildly different from those used by designers working non-digitally today. However, the arrival of digital technology has already had a profound effect on the way print and pattern is created. It is easy to assume that each new technology is more exciting than anything it follows, but there are several reasons for suggesting that as digital printing gradually replaces screen printing, a number of the paradigms at the heart of traditional printed textile design may shift.

Currently, although designers may use digital media to create designs, they almost always have to be separated into a limited colour palette, each component of which is individually rotary screen printed. Furthermore, if this is to be a length of pattern, the designs have to be in repeat. These two constraints, limited colour and repeat, have formed the boundaries of printed textile design ever since production became mechanized; digital fabric printing offers the possibility to free practitioners from the restraints of both.

'Digital imaging has untied our hands with regards to technical limitations. We no longer have to be arbiters of technology; we get to participate in the interpretation of technology into creative content.'

John Dykstra

Digital manufacture

Digital fabric printing is basically an inkjet process. Dyestuff is sprayed onto the fabric by print heads that move from side to side over fabric passing beneath. The most basic printers use a cyan, magenta, yellow and black palette that combine on the fabric to give a broad range of resultant colour. More advanced printers have additional colours to give a fuller colour gamut. The process is controlled by a specialist printer driver called a raster image processor (RIP), which translates the design from file to fabric. Magnified, the resultant design on the fabric can be seen to be made up of tiny specks of each of the dye colours; from any distance, these optically mix to give a full spectrum of colour. The fabric is normally coated with the fixing agent for the dyestuff, unlike traditional fabric printing processes where all the necessary ingredients are part of the print paste applied to the fabric in one go. Some printers are capable of working with pigments that do not need pre-treated fabric.

At present, the process is normally used for sampling or short-run printing. However, new developments include printheads that cover a greater area of fabric with each pass and methods of improving the stability of the fabric as it passes under them. Production plants capable of printing large amounts of fabric at relatively low cost already exist in Asia; it is not presumptuous to predict that the process will gradually overtake rotary screen printing as the dominant mass-production process.

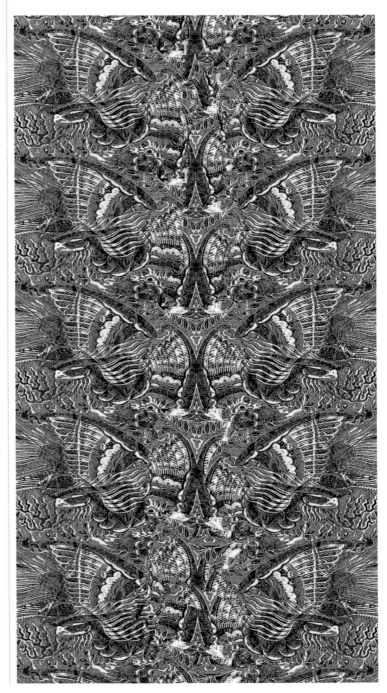

Textile design without textiles

Designers operating digitally have no need ever to come into contact with fabric. A design can be entirely created with software or a hand-made pattern can be digitized via scanning or photography. In either case, the resulting file can be used to digitally print, putting the design on cloth far more quickly than would have been possible with previous printing methods. Most traditionally educated designers would have learnt about screen printing by actually working on fabric; for those on a more craft-based pathway, the print process might have been an integral part of the design process, rather than simply a way to get the design onto fabric once it was finished. In practice, comparatively few designers working in industry (as opposed to designer-makers or similar crafts-focused practitioners) ever work practically with screens and print tables, but the ability to do so was (and often still is) seen as an important part of their design training, not least because it gave them a hands-on sense of working on fabric. It is likely, however, that as digital fabric printing uptake increases, so will print and pattern designers' approach to the actual printing process change, and in particular the role fabric plays. If the designer has any say in the fabric to be used, their engagement with it is likely to be purely down to selection.

This may require a shift in attitudes. It may be contentious to say this, but it is already debatable whether it is worth printed textile design students who want careers as designers in industry to spend much time working with fabric. Most printed textile designers don't get to choose what surface their prints will be on – either this has already been decided before they are given the brief, or they may have no idea who will buy the design. Of course it is important to have an understanding of how print processes work and to have a good basic knowledge of different fabric types, but it is probably more useful to understand how the finished product will work with the design on it. Knowing about how to print onto cotton jersey is arguably less important that being able to visualize how a design on a t-shirt will look when someone is wearing it, particularly when it comes to selling it.

It is important to remember that the technology has to be learnt. It takes a considerable investment of time and effort to get good at painting and drawing – learning software is the same. The building blocks of good printed textile design and colour, drawing, composition and so on apply whatever the media, and are acquired through time and effort. An experienced digital designer may be able to do some things very quickly, but will have put in the graft in order to get good.

Opposite:
Angel Chang collaborated with 3D technologist Adam Beckerman to create this print. It appears cheery and optimistic but the design contains a hidden 3D stereogram of a fighter jet.

Opposite:
A photographic design, put into repeat with software and printed with a digital fabric printer.

Advantages of digital fabric printing

Digital fabric printing offers designers a number of previously unavailable options. Photographic effects and blends from one colour to another are difficult to obtain with screen printing (or earlier methods), but straightforward with the new technology. Colour palettes need no longer be limited – it makes little or no difference to production costs or feasibility if a design has a few colours or millions. The idea of mass-producing designs in unlimited colour palettes is almost impossible with previous technologies.

In addition to the new possibilities that digital fabric printing offers the designer, it does have wider benefits to the production process. There are two areas in particular on which it has a major impact – the time it takes to print a production run of fabric and the ease (and cheapness) of sampling.

With screen printing, there are three main steps between the printer receiving the design and the production run occurring. The design first has to be separated out into its constituent colours, admittedly a process that can be quick if the design is in digital format. Then the screens have to be made and set up to print. Finally a 'strike-off' (a sample of the print) is made and has to be approved before the run starts. This process is considerably shortened with digital fabric printing – the design is sent straight to the printer, and although colour matching can be difficult, it is possible to have a sample within minutes.

The process is far more efficient in terms of dyestuff quantity – with screen printing, only around 60 per cent of the dyestuff actually remains on the textile; the rest is wasted when the fabric is washed out. In comparison, a negligible amount of dye causes an environmental impact with digital printing.

Digital printing offers a level of customization not possible with any other method. Any change in the content or scale of a design can be immediately applied to fabric, and immediately changed back if necessary. Engineered designs can be scaled to suit any size of garment – with screen printing this is normally prohibitively expensive, because a completely new set of screens would be required for every different size. Different elements can be inserted into an existing design with immediate effect. Although the possibilities are nascent and unlikely to be widely adopted for some while, it is possible for the first time to print pattern that operates within set visual parameters, but never actually repeats. Specialist programming creates an image on the fly, arranging an array of elements into a constantly shifting pattern, for example.

Disadvantages of digital fabric printing

There are many advantages to digital fabric printing in relation to screen printing, but there are areas where, at present, the technology lags behind. Large areas of flat colour may have visible banding and the penetration of the dyestuff is not as deep, resulting in noticeably weaker colour on thick or heavy fabrics. Some specialist processes, such as metallic printing, foiling or flocking, cannot currently be done digitally. Any printing process requires the fabric to be prepared in advance, but this is a little more complex for digital printing with dyes, as the fabric often has to be pre-treated with the chemicals required to fix the colour to the fabric.

At present, however, the main reason that digital fabric printing is not more widespread is its relative slowness in comparison to non-digital fabric printing. For manufacturers, major investment is required in moving from screen to digital; this is unlikely to be seen as a viable expenditure until print speeds become more comparable.

The planet

It seems self-defeating in a book on printed textile design to suggest that applying pattern to something does nothing for its function, but merely helps companies increase their profits by selling us stuff we don't really need, using a manufacturing process that probably causes damage to the environment and may involve the abuse of human rights. This, however, is something that practitioners need to face. New designers are increasingly aware of these issues and are keen to change things, but can feel overwhelmed by the scale and long history of the problem. For some time, it has been important for printed textile designers to understand the print process in order to be able to design well for it. It may become increasingly important to know how it works in order to create designs that have a lesser impact on the environment than their forebears.

A need to change

The fashion and textiles industry has a highly detrimental effect on the planet. Broadly speaking, this can be divided into three interconnected areas – the impact on the environment that manufacture and transportation has, the low pay, poor working conditions or other human rights abuses some of its workers have to endure, and forceful marketing that encourages over consumption and waste. When architect Adolf Loos wrote his 1908 essay *Ornament and Crime*, suggesting that it was wasteful to add pattern to products, because it would eventually make them go out of style, he was not referring to the environmental consequences. It could be argued, however, that printed textile designers are employed to create purely superficial designs that add nothing to the function of a product, only serving to fulfil an artificially created want rather than a genuine need.

However, it is important to recognize that print and pattern form a fundamental part of how we choose to express ourselves. The designs we cover our bodies and homes with help to create our identity and form a vital part of our culture. The world would be a dull and joyless place without ornament and many design companies are increasingly aware of the fact that production doesn't have to exploit people and planet. Enjoying our time here doesn't have to mean ruining it for future generations.

'Fashion is eating itself. It has become so disconnected from reality that many of the key issues of our times – such as climate change, consumption and poverty – barely register their presence on the high street or the catwalk. Its products reinforce inequalities, exploit workers, fuel resource use, increase environmental impact and generate waste.'

Kate Fletcher

Despite some concerns that some large companies are merely paying lip service to environmental issues, there are signs that things are starting to change. Even if the willingness to deal with sustainability could be cynically seen to be out of concern for brand identity rather than any heart-felt worry about the planet, businesses are keen to be seen to be acting responsibly. The proportion of start-up companies in the fashion and textiles sector that take an overtly sustainable or ethical stance is increasing all the time. Most importantly, issues that have been seen in the past as being of marginal concern to industry are now being pushed to centre stage, both by new designers who expect their employers or clients to act responsibly and (probably most importantly) by the consumers without whom there would be no industry at all.

DISCUSSION POINT
POLLUTION PREVENTION

The World Bank Group recommended in 2007 that printers use transfer printing for synthetics and digital fabric printing for short runs to lessen the impact on the environment of the textile printing process – both produce less waste than rotary screen printing.

What other steps can you think of that would be viable for mass production, but have a beneficial impact on the environment?

Left:
Luisa Cevese's distinctive bags are made from by-products of the silk manufacturing process that would otherwise have been wasted.

Manufacturing and the environment

It's difficult to think of any stage in the fashion and textiles supply chain that doesn't have an impact on the environment. The fibres used to make natural fabrics are likely to have been grown using fertilizers and pesticides; synthetic fabrics may require the use of non-renewable resources and considerable chemical processing. The process of turning the base fibres or petrochemical product into textiles is likely to require a large amount of energy. Print requires large amounts of water and pollutes with the waste dyestuff and chemicals the process requires – some estimates suggest that up to 20 per cent of industrially polluted water is as a result of textile dyeing or other finishing treatments. Cotton farming requires at least 15 per cent of all the pesticides used on the planet, more than any other single crop. According to the World Health Organization, between one and five million people are poisoned by pesticides every year, 20,000 of whom die as a result.

Manufacturing products from the printed fabric is likely to add to carbon and other environmentally detrimental emissions and the amount of water used. Between each of these stages is likely to be some transportation (between different continents is not unusual), followed by the shipping to the retailer, all of which has a further impact as fuel is used to move them around. By the time it reaches the consumer, a product's manufacture may have involved a journey of thousands of miles and left a big carbon footprint. It can be difficult to get accurate figures on this, but some figures suggest that as many as a third of all people employed in the fashion industry are in logistics – moving things around the planet in the complex route from raw materials to customer.

The role of the consumer

Once the product is in the hands of a consumer, if it has to be washed (as with clothing), this will have a further environmental effect. Water is returned to sewage systems polluted with detergents and most wash cycles involve heating, which adds to carbon emissions. Products that require dry cleaning are no better – a significant proportion of dry cleaners use petrochemical-based solvents that are highly hazardous to the environment.

When the purchaser decides they no longer want the product (not necessarily at the end of its functional life), they may choose not to recycle it or may not have access to the facilities to do this. The product may then end up as landfill, probably taking far, far longer to decompose than it was actually used for. Some printed surfaces can be relatively easily recycled in large quantities – paper giftwrap, for example, or polyester fleece fabrics made from polyester (PET bottles). However, even recycling processes such as these may have an impact on the environment – de-inking (removing printing ink from recycled paper) results in a slurry that may be dumped as landfill (2006 US Department of Energy study). Other fabrics, such as cotton, present far more of a problem, as they cannot be so easily converted into another product. Some design companies have come up with innovative solutions to similar problems, using methods increasingly referred to as up-cycling. Freitag transforms tarpaulins from curtain sided trucks into bags, and waste from local silk weaving companies is used by Italian designer Luisa Cevese for the same purpose.

Left:
Anita Ahuja's company, Conserve India, create individually unique bags from otherwise non-recyclable shopping bags, an item often seen as being symbolic of all that is wrong with current approaches to the environment.

Opposite:
Dutch designer
Hella Jongerious
collaborated
with Unicef and
Ikea to set up a
project combining
small-scale craft
production
and large-
scale industrial
production. The
design shown is
the PS Pelle wall
decoration.

Ethics

Whilst it could be suggested that current concerns about sweatshops and poor working conditions were triggered by the publication of *No Logo* by Naomi Klein in 2000, it doesn't take much digging to find that the fashion and textiles industries have a long history of paying workers tiny wages for long hours in inhuman conditions. Running parallel with campaigns to make industry more sustainable are attempts to make it treat its workers better. Organizations such as the Clean Clothes Campaign strive to improve working conditions in the global garment industry.

An increasing number of new companies are appearing with a philanthropic policy at their very cores. Examples of this include People Tree, who work to Fair Trade principles, use natural dyes, source locally and organically wherever possible, encourage hand-made production (and the training for it) and put funding into local community projects.

Areas of debate

One of the reasons that sustainability is such a hard thing to address is the sheer number of factors involved. Is it, for example, better to use an organic cotton that has to be shipped from the other side of the world than non-organic cotton, grown with pesticides and fertilizers, that has been sourced from closer to home and would therefore leave less of a carbon footprint? And is the genetic modification of (say) cotton such a bad idea if it results in lower use of pesticides? Another area of debate centres on whether it is right to encourage people to keep wearing an individual item of clothing for as long as possible when some research suggests that repeated washing (particularly with biological detergents) can be as harmful to the environment as the manufacturing process.

A difficult balance

Responsibility for poor working conditions or pay cannot always be easily apportioned. A large percentage of companies that use print and pattern don't manufacture their products themselves, but use contractors instead. Large companies that do this often now have clauses in the contract to try and ensure that pay and conditions are of an acceptable standard, but smaller companies are unlikely to have the resources to be able to set this up or police it. Even if such a clause is in place, it is not unheard of for manufacturers to have factories that they show inspectors and others with far worse conditions that they attempt to keep hidden. In order to get the work, some contractors will resort to unethical methods to ensure their profits The issues can be further complicated by regional development agencies or government, who may offer large incentives to companies if they guarantee to manufacture in their area due to the boost this often gives the local economy.

'But now sustainability is such a political category that it's getting more and more difficult to think about it in a serious way. Sustainability has become an ornament.'

Rem Koolhaas

A realistic approach

However strong your ideals when studying, it can be very difficult to put them into practice when faced with the reality of looking for employment. Would you be prepared to turn down a job if it was the only one you'd been offered, but the company involved had some questionable manufacturing methods? It could be argued that it is beneficial to play a part in helping a company with a poor approach to sustainability change for the better. It is ridiculously naïve to assume that you can walk into a job and magically change the way the entire business works overnight, but whether for altruistic reasons or because it may mean a pop at a tax break, the industry is starting to address sustainability issues. All brands care deeply about how they are perceived by their customers. Even if this is for purely profit-related reasons, they want any publicity they get to be positive, and for many businesses, this is increasingly about their attitude to the environment. An awareness of how complex the issue is and some ideas about realistic methods of improving sustainability will improve your employability.

Chapter summary

This chapter's aim was to provide an overview of printed textile design practice. Being able to contextualize your work is a vital part of being a good designer – it should help inspire you, demonstrate that you understand your subject and show you have a clear idea of where your work fits and why. As a professional practitioner, you need to be aware of the history of printed textile design as you may be working with imagery that dates back hundreds of years. If you are preparing for a career, whilst there remains no substitute for experience, an understanding of what you are likely to be doing from day to day is clearly important. Printed textile design exists within a framework of technology that is currently in a state of flux as it becomes increasingly digital. This is nothing to be afraid of; it is exciting and challenging and need not be overwhelming if you are prepared to learn about how to use it. None of this means anything if we don't have a world that treats people fairly and respects its environment; designers have a part to play in ensuring industry is fair and sustainable.

Questions in summary

1. How has history influenced contemporary printed textile design?
2. How has technology influenced printed textile design over the course of history?
3. In which sectors might a printed textile designer work?
4. Which other practitioners might a printed textile designer collaborate with?
5. What change does digital technology bring to printed textile design?
6. How can a printed textile designer attempt to provide sustainable, ethical and responsible design solutions?

Answering the brief

In almost all cases, designers solve problems for people: how can we give this sofa an air of baroque grandeur? How can we sell more t-shirts? Or where can we find some pattern to go on our homeware? The problem is normally communicated to the designer via a brief – a set of requests, reference points or instructions to be transformed into print or pattern.

Designers are paid to answer briefs. If a client asks you to design a small-scale pattern in two colours and you supply a huge design in a mass of colours that you expect them to figure out how to scale down and print, they are unlikely to pay you or use your services again. In simple terms, you are designing what the client wants; the tricky bit is finding out exactly what this is and turning that into designs for print or pattern.

Good practitioners are capable of answering a brief in such a way as to deliver designs that not only fully meet the client's requirements, but do so with creativity, intelligence, originality and style.

This chapter examines the form and key content of the printed textile designer process in order to successfully develop work that meets the criteria of a brief. It looks at the core skills practitioners need in structuring pattern, colour use and product awareness to fulfil the necessary requirements.

The brief

Successfully completing a brief requires all the fundamental printed textile design skills and provides the structure of most professional designers' working lives. There are two simple but highly effective things you can do to help navigate yourself through the process. Firstly, you should try to determine as clearly as possible what the brief is asking you to do, or, if you are writing it yourself, make sure that it will result in the outcome needed. Secondly, you should then answer it. This sounds utterly obvious, but is in fact deceptively difficult. This section will examine what a brief is and a few strategies for working with them.

In most cases, designers answer briefs set (a least in part) by other people. In a professional context, this normally means that the project is set by an employer, an agent or a client. There is a great deal of variation in how this might happen; the designer may have a lot of freedom in how to interpret the project or might be given little room to manoeuvre. The brief might be a very detailed set of instructions with inspirational illustration from the client or a short verbal discussion that the designer is expected to build into the final collection.

Generating briefs

In some cases, practitioners do generate their own briefs. Freelance designers who are representing themselves (rather than working with an agency), will have to do this, often starting by setting their own themes. Experienced print and pattern designers who are in senior positions are likely to have a greater degree of responsibility for each project, often including its authorship. Some employers (particularly smaller ones, or those with fewer products in their range) may expect this and a number of additional responsibilities such as trend forecasting or product illustration from one sole designer. If you are a design student, you will probably find yourself writing your own projects towards the end of your course. As it is likely that your professional career will include doing more than just designing print, you should think about how to extend and contextualize your skills as you do this.

The content of a brief

A brief is a set of instructions to guide a practitioner to a design outcome. It can be very detailed and rich in information or a few spoken instructions; if it is the latter, the designer is likely to spend some time fleshing out a plan of some sort to give enough direction to the creative process. Typically, a brief will have a number of elements within it. Some of these may overlap and they may not be explicitly stated, but you should have an idea about what is required for each of the following items:

Above:
The brief for this wallpaper design was to create a large-scale pattern that was printed in one colour on a grey ground.

Aim
The aim of a brief is generally its overall purpose, expressed in broad terms. This might be along the lines of designing a range of patterns for wallpaper, or creating a collection of prints for swimwear.

Objectives
Objectives can be taken as more specific than aims, and provide more detailed requirements about what is expected. This might be the season the designs are for, for example. In practice, aims and objectives are often lumped together.

Theme or inspiration
These are notions as to how the designs will actually look. They form the visual framework for the designer, and may include text or images as starting points to work from. In most cases, this will give some mention of colour.

Guidelines
These are all the practical things that the designer has to think about when answering the brief. This can include market, product or end-use (including details of the fabric, for example), technical printing details, scale and colour.

Costing
The brief may have to be completed on a budget, or with a specific production cost in mind. This should not be confused with negotiating your fee for the project if working freelance, although this will clearly be reflected in the time you spend on the project and the outcomes of it.

Deadlines
This is the timing of the project. It may be one final point, or feature a number of interim presentations or opportunities for discussion.

Outcomes
This is what the designer is expected to have created at the end of the project. It could be a set number of designs, for instance, with details of the required format. It normally ties the print and pattern in with the product or surface they are for.

The golden rule when dealing with any brief is deceptively simple – answer it. If you only take one piece of advice to heart from this book, make it this: answer the brief.

Client-generated briefs

In a great many cases, designers will be given a brief or project to work to. In this instance, a client-generated brief is just that; one that you haven't written. As a student, your client is your university or college. Your tutors have set the brief (or asked you to write your own) and your response to it will determine your grade. Regardless of how simple or short the brief is, there are some important steps to think about if you want to do your design work well.

Listen

The first, and quite possibly the most important, is to really listen to the client or whoever is setting the brief. If you get the brief in written format, you should go through it very carefully with whoever has set it, making sure you both understand what is required. If you are set the brief verbally, make as many notes as you can, and agree the exact details at the end of the conversation. Following up an initial briefing with a short outline of what was discussed is good practice in any case. Don't assume anything – if there is any room for misinterpretation, clarify things immediately and never feel that it is unprofessional to ask questions. Having said that, the brief may require you to take responsibility for independent thought and creative, original work. You must still answer it; the good practice should be manifest in the way you rise to the challenge.

Plan

The next stage is to plan your time. You should be very clear about the deadlines for the project, which may involve interim presentations or other moments when you have to show or discuss the project. Many designers find it helpful to work backwards from the end of the project, thinking carefully about what they need to have done to be at that point. This should always include the time it takes you to put together your presentation of the work at the end. The more experienced you get, the better you'll know how long it takes you to do each part of the design process and the better you'll get at planning. Always allow contingency time for things going wrong and have back-up plans, particularly if you are reliant on other people or if technology is involved in the process. Of course, the snag with this may be that you are working to a very tight deadline. However, it is much better to say at the start of the project if you think the workload is unrealistic and objectively explain why, than to turn up on deadline day without the thing you were supposed to design.

Once you start working on the project, it is important to keep checking that you are doing what the brief asks of you, particularly with regard to the final product or outcome. The simplest way to do this is to re-read the brief every day, or have it pinned up directly in front of you as you work.

Above:
A quick sketch made in response to a brief to design graphics for men's t-shirts.

Above right:
The sketch was scanned in and used as part of the final design.

Dealing with problems and change

You should also be aware that you may have to deal with negative feedback about the work, or that the brief may change. One of the most popular conversation topics amongst freelance designers (whatever field they are working in) is moaning about clients; this usually revolves around them not making it clear what they want, changing what they want or wanting too much in too short a time. Keeping communication channels open, being professional about criticism and making sure that it is agreed that any changes in the brief may have an impact on time (or payment) at the start can help solve all these problems.

Keeping focussed

Whilst you should always try to answer the brief as well as you possibly can, this is generally about quality rather than quantity. If you have been asked to do something very specific, it is normally better to invest all your time in doing that thing well rather than trying to show a number of choices, none of which may be particularly resolved. Faced with a deadline, you don't want to be giving yourself additional jobs to do. It is important to stress that you may need to come up with a few options for yourself in order to decide the best one for the brief. In professional circumstances, however, you are unlikely to reveal your rejects. In such cases, interim presentations usually involve showing what are essentially fairly resolved final design ideas – the client will want to see how you are going to answer the brief, not merely evidence that you've done some research. This is another big difference between being a student and professional practice.

Self-generated briefs

There are a number of instances where designers themselves may play a large part in setting their own briefs. Senior, experienced designers working for in-house studios may play a large part in deciding the direction of a season's print; freelance designers creating portfolios of work to show prospective buyers will need to focus their design process to ensure it is right for those clients. Although this process may not result in a tangible brief that needs to be understood by others (particularly in the latter case), what the practitioners in question are doing is essentially setting themselves a project. The key to this is knowing where to start (in terms of inspiration and research) and having a clear sense of what will be required at the end.

Particularly when you are first starting out, it can be very helpful to write an actual brief for yourself in these situations. You can use the list of things from the 'The content of a brief' section on page 47 to help with this. The other key factor can be for your research to include examples of how other designers have answered a similar brief. This is not the same as visual research for your inspiration – its function is to give you clues as to how you might deal with whatever the end-use of your designs is going to be, not what they will look like. This is particularly useful if you are designing for a product that you don't have that much experience of working with.

There are many parallels with the authorship, research and development of a brief and trend creation. (The trend creation process is described on page 93.) Although you are ultimately the only person who has to understand a brief you write yourself, the process of writing down what you intend to do can often help crystallize what you need to do. In turn, this can help you keep focused on what you are working on, helping to keep the process on track.

Student briefs

If you are a textile design student, most, if not all, of your study will be centred around projects with some kind of brief. Typically, at the start of your course, the briefs will be quite specific. As your programme progresses, they are likely to become more open as the balance shifts from equipping you with essential skills to your taking more responsibility for the direction of your practice.

Obviously, the standard of the work you produce in response to a student project is used in its assessment. Typically, this happens by looking at all your research, development and final designs to gauge how successful you have been in meeting the learning outcomes or other assessment criteria. To make sure you answer the brief in a professional manner, it is therefore very important to be aware of what these criteria are and to make sure your work shows that you have fulfilled them.

In most cases, college or university briefs run over a longer time than professional ones, particularly in the case of the final major project that many students do; this commonly runs for most of the academic year. Having the opportunity to study in such depth over a sustained period is a wonderful thing and provides the chance to really develop your design practice. To gain experience of working to tight deadlines, you might want to consider either looking for design competitions or including one or more very short projects within your major one. If structuring a short project, this might involve designing a small collection of prints with a different focus from the rest of your work, or with a different product in mind. In either case, this is likely to have the additional bonus of being beneficial when looking for employment – see the section on pages 146-153 about variety of work when building a portfolio.

Above:
Freelance designer Lucy O'Brien created this digital print for a brief she authored herself in the final year of her degree.

AUTHOR TIP
TEN TIPS FOR ANSWERING A BRIEF WELL

1. Make sure you fully understand the brief, and if you don't, ask.
2. Read the brief every day and make sure you stick to it.
3. Recognize that an idea has to be good and appropriate; good alone is not enough.
4. Don't stare into space waiting for inspiration – go and find it.
5. Plan your time. Be realistic. Be very aware of what you have to have done by the deadline.
6. Don't worry if your initial ideas look rubbish. Keep going and they'll get good.
7. Design the print or pattern for the product or end-use. Think carefully about what this means.
8. Look for clues in the way other designers have done similar projects.
9. Knowing what to leave out is probably harder and more important than knowing what to put in.
10. Presentation is vital.

Getting started

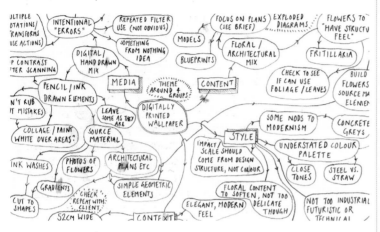

Above:
Mind maps are an excellent way of getting ideas to flow and giving yourself direction at the start of a project.

Opposite:
Inspiration boards not only help to focus on the key images to really kick-start the design process, but can also suggest mixing different source material, an important part of the development process.

No two designers work in exactly the same way, but there are three stages most practitioners go through to get to a final design. The process starts with research - gathering together all the source material, information and sources that the brief needs. This is followed by a development stage, which is essentially the process of experimenting with the research and putting bits of it together to see what works. Finally, the development work is refined into the final designs, deciding what will function best in response to the project. This reflects the way design is taught, although most designers tinker with the process to find a way that works best for them. The boundaries between the three stages often become increasingly blurred. The research process may continue right up to the very end, for example, and observed from the outside, the development stage may seem very short.

In order to find a way to work that best suits your practice, it is important to consider all three stages. In this section, we'll look at the research and development steps; the final design stage will be considered later in the chapter, on pages 68-77.

What is research?

In simple terms, research is gathering together all the stuff you need in order to successfully answer the brief. For a typical printed textiles project, this will involve thinking about a number of different things.

Content

Content is generally the visual information you need to do the project. This can be based around a particular theme - florals, for instance, or geometric pattern. The research process in this instance might involve painting some flowers from life, or drawing some sketches of existing patterns. Crucially, the research process is both finding the source material and working from it. Collecting inspiration is not enough; you have to engage with it, pulling the bits out you need.

The content may be more conceptual - the brief might mention the communication of a particular theme or mood (industrial, say, or pastoral), or concern itself with the reinforcement of the identity of a brand.

Media

These are the techniques or materials used to create the designs, which in turn are likely to be influenced by the method used to print the designs. This might involve traditional techniques such as painting or drawing, or working digitally with a particular piece of software, or any combination of the two. The research process may involve learning how to use a new technique or process, and this in turn may involve a major investment of time. Typically, such experimentation is likely to become development work, sampling ideas for how the final designs might be.

Context

Context is essentially about making sure the design is fit for purpose. It needs to successfully function as print or pattern in end use, as well as appealing to the target demographic. This may involve market research, looking at competitors or building up a customer profile. Thinking about how the design will function in use should be considered from the very start.

Style

Style arches over most of the research - it will reflect the content, the media and the context and may be hard to separate from them. However, it is worth distinguishing, because it may have a crucial role in the brief. For example, the client might want their florals in an art nouveau style, or to have a 1960s retro feel. This might involve some additional research to ensure the imagery used has the style and colour necessary.

Primary and secondary research

Research is often categorized into two types, particularly in academia. Primary research is your own response to things you see. Drawing a bunch of flowers is primary research, as is taking your own photographs of architecture. The key thing here is that it is your own investigation - you are researching by creating work that shows you are trying to find out about what you are looking at.

Secondary research is finding out about what other people have done. This might involve looking at trends or doing market research. Secondary research is very important because it connects your work to the outside world - you can use it to explain why your work is right for its end use.

'...a beginning, a middle and an end, although not necessarily in that order.'

François Truffaut

Opposite:
Sketching out ideas you have thought of as concept drawings or just doodling can be valuable ways of visualising what is in your mind, consciously or otherwise.

Doing research

Research is a balancing act. It should be open enough to look beyond the obvious or the clichéd, but sufficiently focused to avoid wasting time going off on tangents. This is the sort of thing that is always easier to get right in hindsight, and even very experienced designers can spend time doing research that they don't actually end up using. In fact, one of the hardest parts of the design process can be deciding what to leave out; this can be especially tricky if a fair amount of time has been invested in that particular piece of research. In order to refine your own research abilities, try to document your research process, and spend a little time looking back at it after each project you do (this can be part of your sketchbooks or worksheets). You may notice that certain activities prove particularly fruitful – drawings you did from life were much more helpful that ones you did from photographs, for example, or video footage of catwalk shows was more useful than magazine photos. Anything you can do to improve the quality of your research will stand you in good stead for the future.

It is also important to have something to show for your efforts as quickly as possible – there's nothing better for establishing momentum on a project than having a pile of work. It might sound strange, but it is often a good idea not to worry about how a drawing or other visual research looks, particularly in the very early stages – you are not trying to do final designs at this stage. Focus more on trying to work out visually why something has caught your eye, for instance, or getting an idea of how the colour proportions work in the image you are looking at.

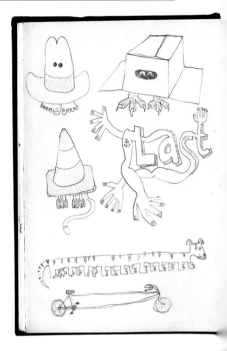

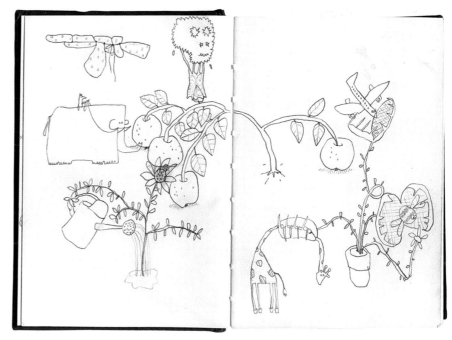

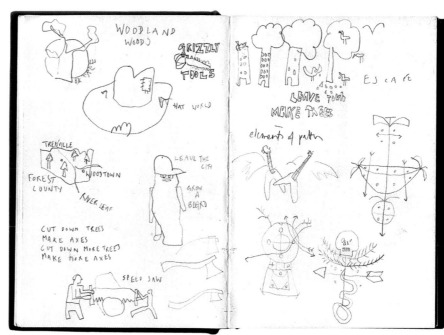

Opposite:
Drawing from life is primary research and a well established step in the design process.

Painting and drawing

Traditionally, drawing is at the heart of the visual research process. Drawing (or painting) in a research context is about asking visual questions. When you draw something, you are finding out all sorts of things about its size, shape and so on, but you are also filtering it through your brain and through whatever media you are working in. You may be trying to find out very specific things about some of an object's characteristics (colour or form, for example), or trying to visualize a concept (an abstract pattern, say).

The process of engaging with what you are looking at or illustrating the idea in your brain is crucial. Even if you dislike what you have done, you should be able to see a way to improve it. The first steps of any project aren't about creating perfectly polished pattern; you are just giving yourself some visual direction.

It is important to understand that anyone can draw. It is difficult, and some people may find it easier than others, but it is a skill that just takes practice to develop. You just need to have the patience to stick at it for long enough to get good. The time investment will pay off handsomely in the long run; the ability to research in this way is probably one of the most important things you can cultivate if you want to be a good print and pattern designer.

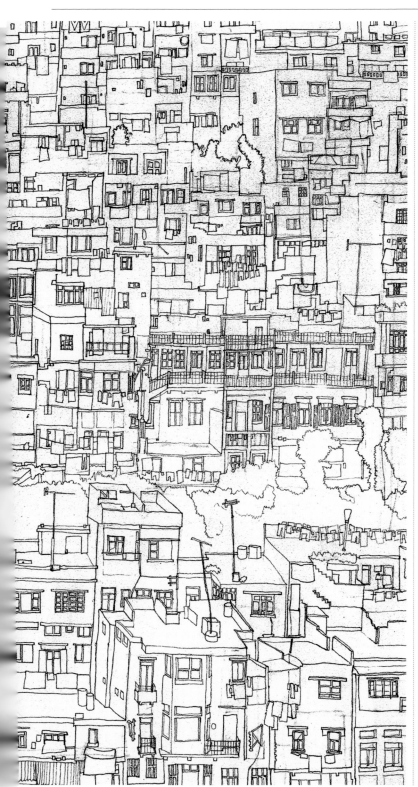

‘My attitude towards drawing is not necessarily about drawing. It's about making the best kind of image I can make, it's about talking as clearly as I can.’

Jim Dine

Painting and drawing with digital media

Digital technology has opened up the possibilities for drawing and painting in a number of ways. Images drawn in traditional media can be scanned in and edited or manipulated. Software can also be used to draw digitally. Using a graphics tablet can have a remarkable effect on the workflow and many designers swear by them.

When researching, it can be useful to think of 'drawing' as another definition of the word: extracting. This is exactly what you should be trying to do at this stage, regardless of the media you are using. You are taking visual information out of your source material or your mind.

Photography

Photography is a very helpful research tool for the printed textile designer. If it is not practical or possible to draw directly from something, photos can be used to work from at a more convenient time or location.

Digital technology offers printed textile designers any number of ways of working with photography, with the boundaries between it and other media becoming blurred or non-existent. Digital fabric printing means that photographic effects are much easier to translate onto fabric than they were with previous printing technologies. The photos you take may be to work with, rather than from.

There are a few things to remember that will help you to get the best out of your photos. Always use the highest resolution or quality available – if you need to enlarge the images later, this will give better results. Think about how you frame your shots. You need to balance getting everything in with being close enough to get the detail you want. Have a spare memory card and battery if possible; running out of storage or charge can be really frustrating. It is also a good idea to get into the habit of organizing your photos. Digital cameras make it all too easy to quickly build up a huge collection. When you transfer the images to your computer, use folders and file names to clearly categorize and label everything you want to keep. Finally, preview the images as you take them to make sure they are in focus and they are lit as you wanted.

Print

Although the Internet has diminished the huge role that books and magazines once played in the visual research process, they still play a central part in the working methods of many printed textile designers. Most collect in two ways. The first is to build up a general library of books, magazines and images they can dip into as needed. In other words, this is stuff that practitioners think might be useful, but don't know exactly what for. The second way is focused to a specific brief, looking for inspiration for a particular subject or theme. This could involve using their own collection, or visiting newsagents, bookshops or libraries seeking very definite things.

As with photography, it is important to have some way of cataloguing this. It doesn't have to be anything fancy; it might be something as simple as a shoe box labelled 'florals' that is full of images of flowers.

It is interesting to note that recent years have seen a large rise in the number of books showing examples of contemporary textile design. In terms of both inspiration and market awareness, these can be an excellent resource (a number are listed in the bibliography on page 195). It is a good idea to look beyond existing textiles, however, and build up a collection from a wide range of visual culture.

If you ever use any found images (or text) in explaining your work to others, you must credit them. Such images should not be used in final designs as this is likely to break copyright law.

The Internet

The Internet is an amazing research tool, but it is also one that does need to be approached with some focus. Faced with the overwhelming amount of information available online, it can be easy to lose concentration when trawling the Internet. Save the URLs of sites you find particularly useful (as Favourites or Bookmarks) and save images you think will be useful as inspiration. As with print images (see above), it is important to be aware of copyright issues, and any images you get online should be credited if shown to others, and not used in final designs.

Because monitors or other displays have a low resolution in comparison to printed material, many images will look better on screen and will not stand much enlargement.

Sketchbooks, worksheets and hard drives

However you go about research, and whatever media or techniques you use, you should make it easy for yourself to access. As a student, you will normally be asked to submit all your research for assessment. Although professional designers may seldom show their research to anyone else, all develop methods to effectively use it. Some people work in sketchbooks, others prefer worksheets. Some people are fine working on screen, others prefer to have things printed out. How you choose to structure your research is down to whatever works best for you, but it is worth taking the time to try different approaches to find the one that works best. It should be easy to navigate (for you, at least) and should do the job of getting you to visually interact with whatever the inspiration or idea is.

If you are working digitally, use folders and filenames to help organize yourself. Simple things like naming images to reflect their content only takes a few seconds, but can save significant time when you're searching for them.

Above:
Taking your own photographs can provide images to paint from or that can be developed digitally into designs.

Right:
Developing ideas
about the scale
of pattern in end
use is best done
by actually placing
onto whatever the
product is. This is
the same pattern
at two different
scales placed
onto a photograph
of a blouse using
Adobe®
Photoshop®.

Professional development

One of the biggest differences between student
design projects and professional briefs is the
attitude to development. In college or university,
it is encouraged to make this as visible as possible,
because it makes it much easier to gauge the
quality of the learning process if the journey can
be seen. This is a good thing; making the process
of developing designs as open as possible makes
it easier to refine and encourages students to
really explore their practice in depth.

However, a professional client's attitude is
likely to be different. They are likely to be far more
interested in the final designs and whether they
fit the brief; they probably don't care too much
about how the work was created. This should
not lull designers into thinking that their working
methods are no longer important. In fact the
opposite is true – to sustain a career in design,
it is vital to have good development skills.

The development process

Development is basically the bridge between
research and final designs. Having gathered all
the visual information you need, you then start
to (say) combine elements for different images,
or re-draw image elements with new techniques.
The shadow of the end-use of the print or pattern
looms large here, and it is important as a
practitioner to keep this in mind to work
effectively on a project.

In practical terms, this means using an
image or sketch of the product that the pattern
will occupy to see how your initial ideas might
work. If you don't know what the product is, trying
out your print ideas on a few likely suspects will
go a long way to help the design process.

Above:
Aware from the start that they would be digitally printed, Frans Verschuren and Patrick Moriarty from the Amsterstampa studio created these scarf designs for their Mokummania collection.

The importance of visual response

One of the key things with development is to give yourself visual options. Don't try and make decisions in your head - always give yourself something to look at. Use this stage to try different things. Bearing in mind time constraints, try to give yourself as many choices as you can and don't be afraid to experiment or take risks.

The development process also needs to take into account the way that the design will be printed. If specified, palettes or limits in the number of colours should be used from the start. If the design has to be in repeat, working with ideas for structures need not wait. Anything that is defined in the brief should create the frame to work within; everything else can be played with.

AUTHOR TIP
KEEPING TRACK OF IDEAS

Ideas about how to develop a project may not hit you as you're actually working on it. At other times, you may be working on one idea when the notion of trying something else springs to mind. At the time, you'll probably think that you won't forget what you thought of, but it is very easy to do this. If you keep a small sketchbook with you, or on your desk as you work, you can quickly note any ideas down, and use them at your convenience.

The other advantage with this system is that the time delay between having the idea and actually doing something with it is likely to give you a better sense of its quality or relevance. It is fairly natural to think all ideas are good at the moment they occur; hindsight is a bit more objective.

Colour

There is an old maxim in printed textile design that you can sell a bad design with good colour, but you cannot sell a good design with bad colour. Whilst it is true that colour should not be seen as separate from the design process (very much the opposite) and that one season's bad colour may be another's good, there is an awful lot of truth in the saying. The brain responds to colour in a very immediate away and in most cases, it is the single most important element of printed textile design.

A colour palette is the collection of individual colours that are used in a design. Typically, a collection of designs will use the same colour palette, although not every design will use all the colours in the palette.

Even if a specific palette is not defined at the start of a project, most briefs are likely to refer to some kind of colour mood or atmosphere; the industry is aware that one of the first things that their customers will register about their products is their colour.

Colour palettes

A colour palette is a group of colours designed to work together. They may be developed alongside the imagery that forms the pattern, although in many cases they may be set as part of the original brief. Colour plays a crucial role in helping practitioners convey a particular theme or concept, and coming up with a well-designed palette that successfully evokes the required mood is a major step in the creative process. So much so, that many printed textile designers treat the palette as the starting point of much of their work.

> **AUTHOR TIP**
> **COLLECTING COLOUR**
>
> Just as you should collect any images you find that you think might inspire you, so you should build up a library of colour. It doesn't really matter what form this takes; just go for any pictures you think might help with developing a palette in future.
>
> Look for a wide range, muted as well as bright, for example, and try to avoid only picking colours or palettes that suit your own personal taste. As a professional designer, you are likely to have to work with a very broad range of colour, some of which you might never choose for yourself.
>
> Try to generate a palette of colour squares (chips) from some of the pictures, or make simple stripes that use the key colours in the same proportions as they occur in the original.

The power of a colour palette in unifying a collection of designs is highly significant. No matter how different the content of the imagery within a collection, if the range uses the same colours, they will invariably work well together.

When designing for particular seasons, colour palettes play a very important role. Typically, spring and summer colours tend to be brighter or lighter than autumn and winter ones. Certain products or markets may also have a particular range of colours associated with them. Swimwear, for example, tends to use brighter colours. It is worth pointing out that there are always exceptions to these rules.

16-1357TC
Orange
Paradiso

19-5513TC
Forest
Night

18-0840TC
Rich
Earth

11-0205TC
Natural
White

16-4728TC
Heavenly
Blue

18-2143TC
Electric
Fuschia

12-07409TC
Faded
Yellow

13-0650TC
Hot
Lime

19-4241TC
Midnight
Secret

14-0852TC
Golden
Oriole

14-6340TC
Ultra
Mint

11-0601TC
Pure
White

14-2808TC
Hydrangea
Base

12-5209TC
Summer
Haze

12-5209TC
Washed
Lavender

Right:
A colour inspiration board, used to develop a working palette.

Far right:
An example of a colour palette, showing the Pantone® reference numbers.

Colour and proportion

It is very important to understand that it isn't only the colours themselves that are crucial to a design. The amount of each colour also has a central role. For example, a colour palette might have a mix of rich, muted colours and acid, bright ones. If the bright colours are used in greater proportion, the resultant designs will look very different than if the muted colours were allowed to dominate. If is fairly common for some colours in a palette to only be used in small quantities – a flash or highlight of colour that is generally referred to as an accent colour.

Linked to this is the role of the base colour of the design. In many cases, designs are printed onto white (or off-white) surfaces. However, some designs may go onto a coloured ground. Ideally, the design should show this. In other words, if you are working digitally and want a design to be printed onto a black fabric, for instance, you should fill the ground of your design with black, ideally as early in the creative process as you can.

Colour and printing

Until the development of digital fabric printing, almost all techniques used to apply colour to fabric did so a colour at a time. A three-colour design to be screen printed needs three screens; a four-colour block print would need four blocks. This means that every additional colour has a significant impact on the cost. In addition to a larger number of dyestuffs, a multi-colour design takes longer to separate into its constituent colours, requires more (say) screens and is harder to align (register). Of course, that is not to say print designs never use a lot of colours, but rather that a brief will typically specify the number of colours a design should use. Knowing at the start of a project that a design is going to be printed with two colours, for example, helps to frame the development process – you don't have to waste time at the end of the creative process trying to get a multi-coloured design to work effectively with a limited colour palette you could have taken into account from the beginning.

Opposite:
Twelve different
screens would
be required to print
the complex colour
effects in this
design, although
the colour appears
fairly simple at
first glance.

Printing colour economically

It is possible in many cases for the base colour
of the fabric or other printing surface to be treated
as one of the design colours. Imagine as an example
a design in red, white and black. Although this
is (obviously) a three-colour design, if the base
fabric is white, the white parts of the design
don't actually need to be printed. In other words,
the three-colour design only needs two screens.

Because digital printing works in a different
way (see page 173), the need to have limited
colour palettes is no longer necessary. Although
their use has evolved partly in response to the
requirements of previous printing technologies,
they have become so central to the printed
textile design process (and such a powerful
method of evoking an atmosphere or look) that
they are likely to remain a crucial element.

Getting consistent colour

Colour matching has long been one of the most
difficult aspects of printing textiles – getting the
final processed colours on fabric to match those
of the original paperwork designs requires a great
deal of skill. Basic colour measurement was made
possible by the development of the colorimeter,
a device which attempts to simulate the way the
eye sees colour. The red, blue and green content
of the sample colour is measured by three separate
detectors. Colorimeters were initially developed
for the brewing industry, as measuring the colour
of beer was seen as a good way of establishing
consistency across different batches of the same
recipe for beer. The technology was quickly
taken up by dyers and printers and subsequently
developed into much more sophisticated digital
devices such as spectrophotometers.

Digital colour matching

Whilst digital technology has solved some
problems, it has also created new ones. One of
the most common is the way different monitors
display colour. If you create a design on your
computer and then e-mail it to someone, it is
likely that their screen will show colour a little
differently from yours – all colour may appear
brighter or warmer, for example. Subtle colours
may look significantly different. Although it is
possible to buy calibrated monitors that ensure
consistent colour display, these are expensive.
The problems can get worse if designs are then
printed out – most people will have had the
experience of the colours looking very different
on paper from how they appeared on screen.
Designers need a way of ensuring that the colour
they are working with is the one the client wants
them to use. When the design goes off to be
printed, the manufacturer must also be clear
about the exact shade required.

Colour referencing systems

The standard way round this is to use a colour
referencing system such as Pantone® or SCOTDIC.
These are highly accurate libraries of colour,
each with its own reference number. Provided
the designer, the client and the printer all have
access to the library, they can all be certain that
they are working with the same colour. For
example, the client could specify that the lime
green they want to use is 13-0650 TC in the
Pantone for Fashion and Home series. The
designer and manufacturer can cross-reference
this with their libraries and be sure they are using
the same green. This doesn't necessarily solve
the problem of how the colour appears on screen,
but it does mean everyone knows what the colour
should be.

Right:

If you look closely at this image, you'll see that it is printed with tiny dots of cyan, yellow, magenta and black ink – CMYK.

Colour theory

There are a few key terms associated with colour theory that can be very helpful for a printed textile designer to know about. They can come in handy when trying to explain verbally explain how you want a colour to be altered, for instance, or how it should look in comparison to another colour.

Hue

Hue is a measure of where a particular colour sits in the spectrum. Orange, red and purple are all expressions of hue.

Tone

Tone is the lightness or darkness of a colour. White is the lightest tone and black is the darkest; yellow is a lighter tone than ultramarine. Light tones of a hue may sometimes be referred to as tints, with dark tones referred to as shades.

Saturation

Saturation is a gauge of how pure a hue is. Cyan (process blue) is a very saturated colour, whereas grey is a completely desaturated colour.

Another colour theory concept can be helpful in understanding how colour functions when printed as opposed to how it appears on a screen or monitor.

Additive colour

Colour can occur in two ways. It can be additive, which means it comes from a light source - the sun, say, or the screen on your phone. Because the light is being produced from an object, it is also known as emitted colour. The more emitted colours you combine, the lighter and brighter the result. White light contains all the colours of the spectrum mixed together. Monitor screens are made up of tiny red, green and blue light sources (hence RGB). If all three are on in a particular area, this will be seen as white. Combining just red and green light will give yellow, red and blue will give magenta and green and blue will give cyan.

Left:
This design was
created with an
unlimited colour
palette for use
as a digital print.

Subtractive colour

Colour can also be subtractive. This means that
you can only see it as the result of reflected light.
The words you are reading now are subtractive
colour. Light from the sun or a bulb hits the page
you are looking at. The white of the page reflects
most of this light back; the black text reflects very
little. The page needs an external light source to
reflect off it to be seen; for this reason, subtractive
colour is also known as reflected colour. The
images in this book are made up of tiny dots
of cyan, magenta, yellow and black ink (known
as CMYK). Seen from a distance, the dots merge
to give a full range of different colours, an effect
known as optical mixing. Physically mixing
subtractive colour results in darker, desaturated
colour - mixing green and red paint, for example,
would give a brown.

Digital fabric printers print with tiny drops
of dye in a limited range of colours. Although they
may mix physically a little when they first hit the
fabric, the resultant colour is essentially optical
mixing - if you look very closely at the surface
of a digitally printed fabric, you can see little flecks
of colour.

Final designs: repeat and placement

As the design process unfolds, the experimentation of the development stage gives way to refinement. As a designer, you start to decide which ideas work best and how you can use them to answer the brief.

There are any number of methods that designers can use to help create final designs. Most practitioners develop a range of their own processes over time, often subconsciously refining their techniques as they work on design after design. Ultimately, the way to get good at doing it is to do a lot of it, but there are some useful tips to help you get to grips with the process, and this section will look at a few of them.

A final printed textile design has to satisfy a number of needs. It must look good, answering the visual requirements of the brief. Linked to this is its appeal to its target customer. It must be printable, using a specified number of colours if the client so wishes. It must function in use – the scale and proportion of the design, for instance, should work on the final product. Practitioners have to balance all these things. Even if they are creating designs that don't yet have a known client, having an idea of all these needs will help to make the final design more sellable.

'The repetitions of patterns give us rest. The marvels of designs stir the imagination.'

Oscar Wilde

Refining designs digitally

Digital technology has had a very large impact on the way designers work. The speed and ease of editing designs is significantly increased by working with computers, although a big chunk of time needs to be devoted to learning how to use the software to really take advantage of it. From a printed textile design standpoint, one of the most useful features of image editing is the ability to work on individual parts of a design without affecting the rest. Using Layers in Adobe® Photoshop®, for example, means motifs can be quickly and independently edited, leaving the rest of the design untouched.

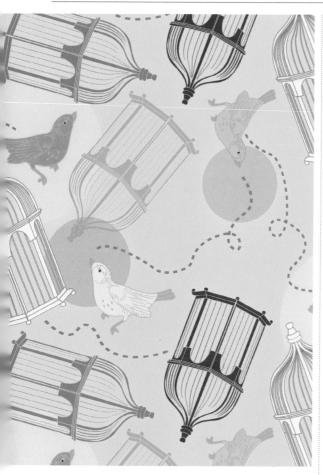

Working with repeat and placement designs

Printing is essentially a process of being able to repeatedly transfer the same image. The image can be a single image applied once to each surface (as in a t-shirt motif), or it could be designed to cover a very large surface (like a roll of wallpaper) with pattern. Such a design is known as a repeat, all-over or tiled design and this process has been at the heart of printed textile design for much of its history. In this section, we'll look at some of the basic methods of creating good repeat designs and introduce some of the structures designers use.

Repeat and placement for different markets

It is important to note that at lot of designs created for use in fashion, particularly when not created in-house, give a suggestion of repeat rather than a millimetre perfect, fully resolved design ready to print. This, along with the smaller scale of the designs, may go some way to explain why they sell for significantly less than their furnishing counterparts. It is rare for designs destined for the home / interior market not to be created in full repeat, and if you are working for this market, it will be taken for granted that you can design in repeat.

Understanding how repeat and placement designs work

At first, creating a placement print seems very simple in comparison to creating a repeat. The design is just an image that (almost) always gets printed in exactly the same place on its product. However, in many cases, there is a real art to doing this well. Crucial to this is an understanding of how the design and the product interact – where will the design go, for instance, and what size will it be? Whilst it is true that there tends to be little variation of this with some products (t-shirts, for example, very often have the print in the middle of the chest on the front), it is good to develop an awareness of designing with the end-use in mind. In some cases, this may help to sell the design.

Unless you are told otherwise, final designs are always done at the size that they will be printed. If, for example, you are working digitally on a 32cm x 32cm (12.6in x 12.6in) design, the file must be this size when printed. Resolution is also important for computer based designing; again, unless you are told otherwise, work at 300dpi.

Left:
This design by Claire Roberts is in half drop repeat.

Repeat and placement terms

There are a number of technical terms associated with designing that are useful for printed textile designers to know.

Motif or element

A single part of the whole design. In a repeat design, a motif may be an individual unit of the pattern. A seven-element floral repeat would be one that is made up of seven different flowers.

All-over

Common alternative term for repeat, sometimes automatically used to refer to a multi-directional repeat. Tiled can also be used, although this may specifically refer to a block repeat.

Multidirectional

A repeat that works when viewed from any angle – in other words, it has no noticeable top, bottom, left or right. (This is normally achieved by rotating the elements that make up the design to a variety of different angles.) It is favoured by cost-conscious manufacturers because pattern blocks can be placed anywhere and at any angle on the fabric.

Bi-directional

A repeat that has an interchangeable top and bottom; a stripe is the most basic example of this.

Block repeat

The most simple repeat structure, a block repeat pattern does the same thing directly beneath itself and directly to the side. The structure is a simple grid. Despite the straightforwardness, it can be very easy to spot the horizontal and vertical structure, especially from a distance. It takes a skilled designer to create a good block repeat.

Half drop repeat

A half drop (also known as a step) repeat is a design that repeats directly beneath itself, but drops down by half its height to the side. If you look at a brick wall turned through 90° (turn your head so it is on your shoulder), that is a half drop structure. This is the most commonly used repeat, particularly in fashion. The design can step down by different amounts to the side – a third drop would go down by a third of its height, a quarter drop by a quarter and so on.

Brick repeat

A brick repeat goes directly to the side, but moves across by half its width as it goes downwards. It is relatively uncommon in use.

Spot repeat / sateen repeat

A design where an element (or combination of elements) is arranged to appear randomly scattered within a square, often with each rotated at a different angle. The whole square is then repeated, normally in block or half drop.

Turnover or mirrored repeat

The design is flipped horizontally or vertically to get the repeat structure. Digital editing makes this very easy; doing it well is difficult.

Border

A border is a relatively narrow design that runs around the edge of a garment, say, or along a specially designed thin stripe of wallpaper. Borders normally only repeat side to side. In some cases, the design may be printed down the fabric, which is then turned through 90 degrees. This is known as 'width for length' printing.

Repeat size

This is the distance down or across from any point on a design to where the same thing occurs again. If only one number is given, it will be the vertical repeat size; two is horizontal as well (but if they are different numbers, check which is which). The repeat size is governed by the technology used to print it. With a rotary screen, for example, if the circumference of the screen is 64cm, the repeat size will be 64cm or a division of that (32cm, say, or 16cm).

Although certain sizes do crop up a lot, there are a large number of repeat dimensions that get used and you should always check that the brief gives the sizes you have been asked to work to. The wallpaper industry, for example, typically uses different sizes from fashion. Always check the unit to see if it is centimetres or inches.

Left:
This design is in brick repeat.

Designing in repeat

A good repeat is sometimes referred to as a balanced design. When seen over a large expanse, no single element, or gaps between any elements, will stand out. The longer it takes to find the repeat, the better it is. It is very difficult to generalize about the process as every design is different. However, it is generally a case of trying to conceal the repeat by arranging the elements in such a way as to prevent any one or any gaps between them from dominating. If one motif does overshadow the others, the eye will tend to see the structure of the repeat rather than the pattern within it.

Designing in repeat can be helped by understanding a few principles and structures, but the best way of getting to grips with it is to physically create a design and move the elements within it about by eye. It is important to try and avoid obvious verticals or horizontals (the human eye will naturally notice these) and, with multi-element designs, to make sure one motif doesn't outdo the rest. As with many other design techniques, the best way to get good at it is to do a lot of it. It is a strange mix of practising a lot, yet remaining intuitive to what is happening in front of you.

The following tips should help you to design in repeat, but be prepared to abandon any rules if you think the design looks better without them.

AUTHOR TIP
LOOKING FOR REPEAT

Get into the habit of always trying to spot the repeat whenever you see a new pattern. If you are clothes shopping, for instance, look at printed textile designs and have a go at working out what the repeat structure is and how big it is. Look at an element of the design and then go down the fabric (or other surface) until you find the element repeating. Do the same thing to the side.

Always work in repeat from the start

It is almost impossible, even for very experienced designers, to see what is happening in a design if you can only see one unit of it. It is much better to set up a two-by-two version; you can see four units at once and although it is a bit slower to get started on, it will save considerable time in the long run. Working digitally makes it very easy to duplicate elements. Set up a file that is twice the width and height of your repeat. Every time you bring a new element into the design, copy it so you get four identical versions and put one in each repeat unit, so you get two horizontal and vertical repeats. This way you can immediately see what is going on with the repeat – just be aware that you may need to spend time going between the different elements to move them if the design has quite a few in total. Traditionally, repeat designs showed about 5cm (2in) of the repeat on the bottom and one side, but this dates back to when they were always hand painted and it would have been highly time consuming to work with more of the pattern in repeat.

Look at the repeat from a distance

To see if any element is standing out too much, see what happens if you zoom right out from the image, or look at it from across the room. Do this regularly - don't wait until the design is nearly finished. If something does dominate, try making it smaller, more subtle in colour or partially covering it with something else. What the negative space (the gaps between the motifs) does is as important as what the motifs themselves do.

Get good at half drops

There are a large number of repeat structures beyond the ones mentioned in this book, but the most common is the half drop. A large part of its popularity stems from the structure making it relatively easy to hide obvious horizontals. New practitioners tend to start by working on block repeats, which, although the structure is simpler, are less forgiving and less common. By all means try both, but practise half drops a lot.

Use more elements

Putting a single motif into repeat is obviously quite limiting. You will learn about repeat faster in the long run if you work with designs that have at least five or six different elements. Bring them in one at a time, put them in repeat and adjust their position as you go. Clearly there will be times when you might be asked to work with just the one or two motifs and you should practise that too, but the sooner you get going with more complex content, the better.

Left:
Creating a half drop – this sequence of images shows a number of steps in the creation of a half drop design.

Placement and engineered prints

A placement or engineered print is a design that is not in repeat and that is normally applied to the product in exactly the same place. An example is a graphic on a t-shirt; the design will be printed on (say) the chest of the garment, and will, in almost all cases, be placed in the same position.

Although the definitions are a little cloudy, a placement print is a fairly generic term that generally refers to any design that occupies an identical location. If the design is on fabric, it could be printed onto a length of cloth before the product is made. However, in many cases (such as the t-shirt example), it is printed after the basic product is manufactured. It is not necessary to know the exact shape of the surface that the design will be printed on.

The word 'engineered' may be used to refer to a design that is applied to the substrate before it is made into the product. The term is derived from the way that the print or pattern is engineered to be printed so the designers know exactly where it will go once the product is made up. In a fashion context, an engineered print could be designed for two adjoining blocks (pattern pieces). When the garment is assembled, the design appears to flow uninterrupted across the seam that joins them. In this case, knowledge of the shape of the surface is vital, particularly if the product is three dimensional.

For the sake of explaining how to design in this way, these definitions will be used, but you shouldn't be overly concerned with the exact meaning as this may be interpreted differently by different clients. The key thing to be aware of is the difference between designing with or without needing to be aware of the exact dimensions of the product or its components. However, remember that even if you don't know the exact dimensions, you need to know enough to be able to design with a good idea of where you want the final design to go on the product and how this will look.

Designing for product

Whilst it is not necessary to know the exact size of the product, it is important to have some idea. As with the exercise on the previous page, you can take measurements off a similar product that you own or have access to. You should then work full scale when doing the final design, and, if you are working digitally, at 300dpi unless told otherwise.

It can also be useful to see how the design looks on the product as part of the design process. Some methods of illustration pattern in end-use are given on pages 96–101 – even a quick sketch can be really useful to check that the design works effectively. If you are working on a design for an engineered print, knowing the exact dimensions is vital.

More than one set of measurements may be needed – if a garment is made in several sizes, or a roller blind has different lengths or widths, you may be required to do different versions of the same design to suit the product range. The process can be further complicated by changes in scale during the manufacturing process. If a designer is creating an engineered print for fabric, the finishing process is very likely to alter the dimensions of the design – a process that generally involves steaming (to fix the dyestuffs) and washing (to remove any excess colour) is highly likely to shrink the base textile, very often to different percentiles in width and height. In practice, the high production costs mean that this is fairly unusual, but it has got easier with advances in digital technology and it is worth having at least a cursory understanding of how to deal with such design problems.

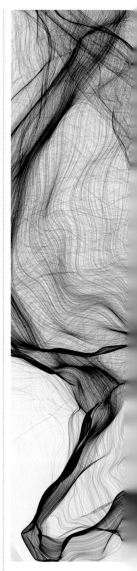

Above:
Eno Henze 'Green Ambush' wallpaper for Maxalot. A very large-scale placement print, this wallpaper is digitally printed so the design runs perfectly across each roll to make up the full image.

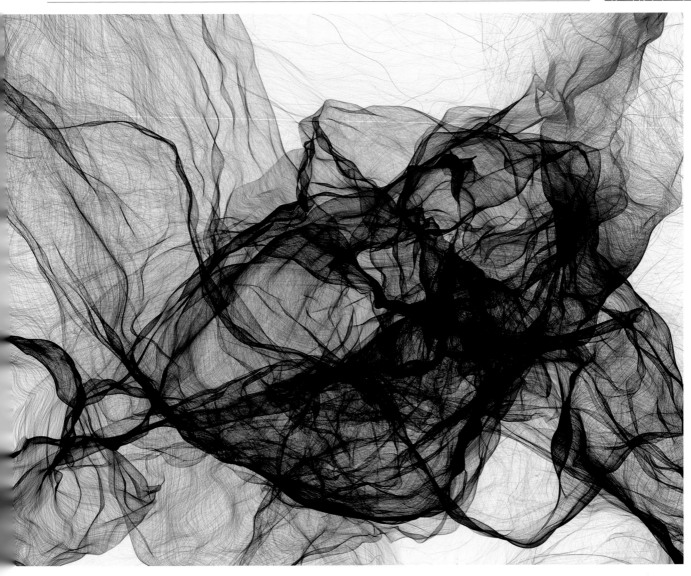

Right:
A photograph by Solve Sundsbo has been engineered to go in a specific place on this Surface2Air garment.

DISCUSSION POINT
DESIGNING A T-SHIRT GRAPHIC

Lay one of your own t-shirts out flat and take enough measurements from it to be able to draw it accurately.

Working either on paper or digitally, use the dimensions to create a full size template of the tee.

Now create a graphic for the garment, working directly into this shape and using it to judge where to place the elements of your design.

Try to be aware of working to the product shape rather than working within the rectangle of a piece of paper or window on screen.

Experiment with moving your design around inside the template and, if possible, changing its scale.

Every time you see a t-shirt (or any other product) with an unusual placement print position, make a sketch of it and add it to your inspiration library.

Right:
Henrik Vibskov 'Flimono' dress S/S 2010. The print design on this garment is engineered to fill the sleeves, shoulders and skirt.

Satisfying manufacturing needs

When you create a final design for printed textiles, you are essentially creating a set of instructions. The printer will use your design to apply pattern to fabric or other surface. The final design should therefore be an accurate representation of what you and your client want printed. The scale should be correct, with the design shown the same size as it would be printed. The colour should accurately depict the actual colours to be used, if necessary using a reference system to provide a cross reference. The number of colours used is also a vital consideration if the design is to be screen printed. If the design is in repeat, it should be precise and designed in such a way as to allow the pattern to flow down the fabric, apparently unburdened by structure.

It is also vital that the design is created with the product in mind. Even if it is not required as part of the brief, the process of visualizing the pattern or print on the product helps both your creative process and the client's understanding of how the final design will function. Contextualizing your work properly right from the start ensures that the relationship between the design method and its end use is harmonious and will make you a better practitioner.

Left:
Jonathan Saunders

'Always design a thing by considering it in its next larger context – a chair in a room, a room in a house, a house in an environment, an environment in a city plan.'

Eliel Saarinen

Chapter summary

This chapter has sought to provide a broad overview of the process involved in the research, development and creation of a final printed textile design. As you gain experience, you will find your own ways of doing this; there is no substitute for practice here. Every time you create a new final design or collection, you will become a better designer, particularly if you take a moment or two after you have finished to go back over the process and analyse how you did at each stage. If you did things well, try to work out why, and make sure you build on them in future. If some parts of the process proved more of a challenge, ask yourself how you could improve them and prevent the same problems arising again.

At the heart of this chapter has been one idea – to try and encourage you to work as if you were a professional designer from the very first moment you start to design printed textiles. Even if you can't deal with all the different factors involved in successfully answering a real-life brief at first, having a sense of the direction you need to move in and the things your practice should include will help you develop into a designer who is both creative and professional.

Questions in summary

1. What are the key elements of a design brief and what is its purpose?
2. What steps should a printed textile designer undertake to ensure they fully answer a brief?
3. How might visual research be carried out?
4. How can research ideas be developed and refined into final design?
5. What role does colour play in printed textile design?
6. Why is it important to have an idea of product or end-use when designing?

Context & communication

This chapter will look at the place print and pattern has in the wider world and why this is important for practitioners to know about. In order to function effectively, designers have to be able to demonstrate they have taken a number of factors on board to show their work is fit for its end-use. In practical terms this comes down to two things: context and communication.

The context of a design is the relationship it has to the world around it. It relates to the product, the person who might buy the product, how industry will manufacture it and the styles that the design might draw upon.

Having an understanding of the various contexts within which a design will exist is one thing, but just as important is the ability to communicate this. Often, this is a case of helping to make the employer or client feel confident that the design will do the job it is supposed to. Communication may also be part of a brief. Printed textile designers may be asked to reflect a brand's core values in their work, or even contribute to the styling or art direction in the marketing of a product. The design industry is not static; its structure changes all the time and recent years have seen an increase in designers working across a number of separate disciplines. Knowing that your work might be of interest beyond traditional sectors, and what might be required to get work in these areas can be really useful.

Industry criteria

Above:
As manufacturing lead times decrease and customers expect new product more than twice a year, many observers predict that the old two season industry structure will eventually disappear. This design by Liliane Bomestar from Dutch studio Amsterstampa could be used for either Spring / Summer or Autumn / Winter.

Seen as a whole, the industry works along broadly similar models. Although there may be variations with individual companies, particularly those in different sectors such as fashion or furnishing, certain key criteria are used by almost all employers or clients that printed textile designers are likely to find themselves working for. Factors such as season, the use of trend predictions or forecasts and the marketing of design products to specific target customers are standard practice. At the very least, designers need to know about how these things work; if you are looking to raise your employability, being able to turn your hand to areas of design beyond straightforward print and pattern could be a skill worth pursuing.

Season

The fashion and textiles industry generally operates seasonally. There are a number of reasons for this, particularly in the clothing industry, as people need cooler clothes in summer and warmer clothes in winter. Most retailers, especially those in the fashion sector, have major stock updates twice a year (normally following the sales). In practice, many retail companies also introduce new stock throughout the year, but the significant change twice a year still prevails. Catwalk collections and trend publications, for example, are either Spring/Summer or Autumn/Winter (Fall/Winter in the US). While furnishing companies may not be quite so sweeping in their updates, they will follow cycles of introducing new ranges, and there are certain products (such as garden furnishings) that may be very seasonal.

From the perspective of the printed textile designer, probably the most important consideration with regard to season is colour. Spring/Summer palettes tend to be brighter and lighter than Autumn/Winter ones. Certain sectors of the market sell in considerably greater quantities at certain times of the year, swimwear being an obvious example.

Although sectors within the industry do tend to follow similar calendars (see page 91), freelance designers working across diverse areas may find themselves working on different seasons in close succession. Even though trade fairs may target a specific season, for example, buyers attending them may be looking for print and pattern for a different point in their production cycle, and exhibiting studios are unlikely to show solely (say) Spring/Summer designs.

'People ignore design that ignores people.'

Frank Chimero

Trend prediction and forecasting

Originally, new ideas and inspirations filtered through the industry in a fairly linear way. The innovation happened at the top end of the market and companies at lower levels took their lead from above, adapting the designs to suit their customers and budget. Haute couture fashion houses, for example, sold seats at their shows for large sums of money to companies catering for mass markets, sometimes even offering mock-ups of certain garments in paper or calico. Unofficial drawing or photography would be forbidden, and those permitted to take photos would not be allowed to publish them until the couture customers had their clothes or the mass market clients had started the production process.

In the 1960s, designers began to create designs that looked away from the high end for inspiration and the whole structure of the business began to grow more complex. Mass market manufacturers realized that the traditional filtering-down of designs from above tended to create designs that looked old fashioned in comparison with the work the new designers were doing. Forecasting companies began to appear offering manufacturers a service in finding out new trends and inspiration, often drawing on sources from all over the world. Printed textile design was very much a part of this, with the forecasters providing trends in pattern and print as a key element of their service.

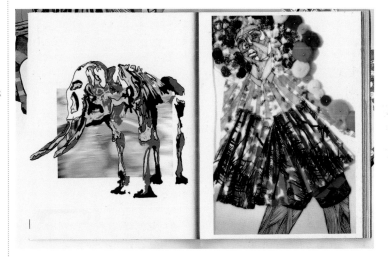

Trend timing and content

The term prediction is a bit of a misnomer; in fact the companies that do it are essentially offering a direction and inspiration service. Trends are normally produced seasonally, with most print-based suppliers offering two publications a year. This is normally a Spring/Summer and Autumn/Winter edition, each providing trends for a point roughly two years in advance. Recent years have seen a rise in subscription-based services to web-based trend information, which can be constantly updated. In addition, some trend companies offer a consultancy service, providing trend information tailor-made to a particular clients' needs.

Above:
A spread from Emmanuelle Sayer's Cruel Carnival trend, created as part of a student project.

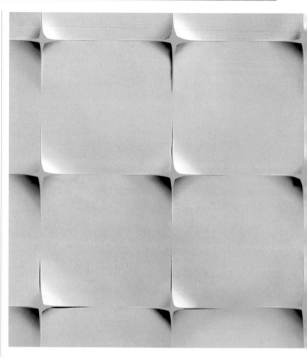

Above and right:
This two-dimensional design for furnishing fabric, by Alexandra Devaux for Creation Baumann, appears three-dimensional.

Working with trends

From a printed textile point of view, trends can have a number of roles in a designer's work. Practitioners working for an in-house studio may find that their employer buys or subscribes to one or more trend prediction services, which they will encourage their design staff to use as part of the creative process. Broadly speaking, these lie along a scale with two extremes. At one end are the most esoteric, based around fairly abstract concepts that offer a wide range of possible interpretations to the designers who use them. At the other end are the much more straightforward, which are almost like instructions and may even come with elements that can be cut and pasted to quickly create designs. All will include colour palettes (or at least colour moods) and most will have some notion of how the designs would work on an end product. Some focus only on print and pattern, while others might deal with a whole production sector such as menswear or interiors (these will be focused on a particular market, however).

In some cases, printed textile designers may create their own trends. This might be part of their job description if they are working for an employer, or something they do on a more informal basis if they are freelancing and want to keep their work fresh. Finally, some trend agencies may use print designers to create or report on trends for them as part of their service.

One thing to be aware of is that when mainstream magazines talk about trends, they are normally referring to products that are already in production. Their writers are looking at products or previews (such as fashion shows) and trying to spot similarities between different brands. These are trends for consumers, not designers, although practitioners are likely to be aware of them and they may have some influence on the design process.

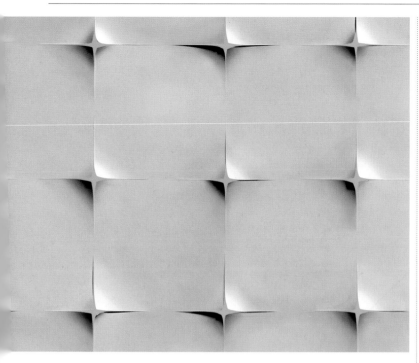

All this means that the print or pattern has to be demonstrably aware of its projected customer. If the designer is working for a specific client or employer, the print and pattern should obviously fit the needs of their market. Being able to show this is a highly effective skill for print and pattern designers. Creating a presentation board or slide that reveals your design process has been underpinned by market and customer awareness can really help convince your audience of your collection's worth.

There are a number of strategies for going about market research, but there are a few key things to help get started. If you are designing for a specific company, you should clearly look at what they do, ideally over a couple of seasons or ranges. You should also focus on the specific sector you have been asked to design for - womenswear, say, rather than all fashion, or blinds rather than all soft furnishings. It is also a good idea to look at competitors for that market. This can be a bit confusing, but if you look at the price point of a fairly standard item (a little black dress, for example) and then find other companies who are selling that product for the same sort of price, they will be aiming at the same sort of market. Note that expensive markets have a far broader range of prices than cheaper ones.

Targeting customer and market

At the heart of any business plan is the notion of being able to demonstrate that the product has a market. Any company in the fashion and textiles sector will try to establish a clear understanding of what it is customers want, and the print and pattern it covers its products with will reflect this. Seen purely from a marketing perspective, printed textile design is a way of adding value to a product or increasing its appeal to a particular customer. With many products, the design may be crucial to why people buy it. Although it may do nothing for it is function, it becomes a vital characteristic and hence central to making it appeal to its target audience and how it is marketed.

Opposite:
Carmen Woods'
'Made of Wood'
collection uses
hand-drawn
elements with an
illustrative style.

Doing market research

Once you have established a few competitors at the same level, you can then look at how they use print and pattern in comparison. It is also very worthwhile to look at a few brands who you think may influence your market – typically these will be at a higher level, although this isn't always the case. This needs to be focused, but with a big of digging, you should be able to establish which companies are using print in a particularly influential manner.

Sometimes, the complexity of the print may have a bearing on market level, but this isn't always the case – it is possible to spend a fortune on products that have a simple one-colour print, and equally possible to pick up cheap products that may feature a lot of different colours and more than one technique. The quality of the material the product is made from and its construction are likely to be a much better indication, but this requires quite a lot of experience and knowledge and can be difficult to do in a shop environment, and impossible if researching online.

It is also very important to look at the way the brand projects itself to the outside world. This normally involves looking at three things – retail environments, websites and advertising. Obviously, if the brand is one that only sells online, the first two overlap. Companies spend a lot of time and effort on the styling and visual merchandising of their products, and the way they do it speaks volumes about their markets. Simple things like the amount of product in the shop are very revealing – brands at the lower end of the market will pack as much product in as they can; high-end brands may have very little stock in the shop at all.

Producing designs for different end uses

Printed textile designers' careers may take them in a variety of different directions, working for a range of sectors within the industry.

Each sector has different requirements; there are particular influences on each and needs that have to be considered when designing for them. Attempting to definitively categorize all the areas of the design world that a printed textile design could foreseeably work for is very difficult, but there are some overarching definitions that are in common use in industry.

Fashion

There are a large number of different ways that the fashion world can be divided. The three most frequently named sectors are probably menswear, womenswear and kidswear. In turn, these can be targeted at specific types of garment such as sportswear, jeans or casual wear and formal wear.

Colour and imagery play a big part in differentiating between the end-uses, and the role that printed textile designers have can be pivotal in targeting a particular sector. Menswear tends to be more muted in colour than womenswear, for example, and florals are used far more sparingly for men than for women.

The age of the target customer also has a big effect in fashion. Many high street brands focus on 18 to 30 or 35 year-olds, not least because they are likely to spend more on clothes than any other age group. Print designs for this market are likely to be more trend aware; those aimed at an older market may require a more timeless, classic look.

Furnishing

The home and interiors market can also be divided into a large number of sectors. These may relate to the customer - home furnishings for the domestic consumer, contract furnishing for business use such as workplaces or hotels. Some furnishing companies deal with very focused product ranges such as tableware or carpets and floor coverings, whereas others may operate within the whole of a much broader sector such as homewares. Sector names may be used by some companies to differentiate themselves from others who have a very different style - fashion interiors implies something much more contemporary than soft furnishings.

Because people tend to update their interiors much less often than their clothes, trends in the furnishing sector tend to move more slowly than in fashion, often paying heed to previous season's styles to a larger degree than their apparel counterparts. Indeed, print or pattern designs that sell well may be kept in a range for years, possibly being updated with new colourways from time to time. The exception to this is often smaller, relatively cheaper homeware products such a china or lighting. These may be targeted at younger people (especially those in rented accommodation) who will be less likely to spend heavily on major decoration or furnishing, but willing to spend on smaller items to personalize their homes.

Giftware and stationery

Print and pattern are used heavily in these sectors and although the product concerned is unlikely to be fabric based, many designers working in this area are from a printed textiles background. Others come from illustration or graphic design training; the wider range of practitioners working in these fields is sometimes reflected in the way freelance designers sell to them. Licensing designs for a fixed period of time or for a single specific use is relatively common in comparison to the way designs are sold to the fashion and furnishing sectors, where it is normal for copyright to be sold in perpetuity.

Some companies work on very specific areas such as giftwrap or cards, while others work across a broader range, possibly overlapping with furnishing or fashion.

The bigger picture

In the previous section, we looked at how an understanding of what is happening within the industry is important for printed textile designers. This world sits within a much bigger one – one that affects and influences it in all sorts of ways. For example, the financial crisis that began in the US banking system in 2007 had a significant impact on retail, as many people saw their disposable income fall. The market for non-essential items became more competitive; most products that printed textiles designers work for fall firmly into this camp. Environmental and sustainable issues have also begun to impact on the choices customers make, the effects of which ripple through to the way print and pattern is designed and used on products.

It is also important for designers to be aware of cultural changes around them. Although some printed textile work is very self-referential, many of its practitioners draw on a wide range of reference points from other areas of visual culture and beyond.

Technical advances are also likely to have an effect. As we can see elsewhere in this book, digital fabric printing has the potential to significantly change the way that designers can work.

Over the next few pages, we'll look at how to develop a basic understanding of the way these external factors affect printed textile design. This is powerful knowledge to have when it comes to explaining why your work is right for a particular client or product.

AUTHOR TIP
INNOVATION VERSUS
COMMERCIAL SUCCESS

Ground-breaking textile design tends to be more influential than commercially successful – it can take a while, particularly in the furnishing sector, for customers to be sufficiently at ease with a new design trend to be willing to let it in their home. History often remembers the critically acclaimed or prize-winning designs and not always the ones that were bought in quantity. In many ways, this is a good thing, but it does serve to highlight the fact that it can be difficult to earn a living in this area of design by innovation alone.

Do you think this an inevitable part of a design process that is part of a much wider business?

Can you find examples of designers or companies who manage to combine genuine innovation with commercial success?

The calendar

Before looking at the bigger picture, there is another industry factor to consider - the calendar that much of it works to. This is of considerable importance to printed textile designers as it means they will often be creating pattern for between a year and a year and a half in the future.

Although the industry is getting faster all the time at getting product designed, made and into shops - some companies boast of a lead time of six weeks - it is built on the back of a system that allowed over two years for the process of getting from yarn production to the customer buying the final product. Originally, this meant that particular sectors of the textile industry almost all did the same things at the same time. The timing of trade fairs, for example, is aimed at particular moments in the production calendar when buyers or studio directors might be looking for designs.

Timing

Once designs have been bought, time is needed to perform any adaptations or alterations necessary before the designs go off to the printer. Fashion designs that have been bought with a suggestion of repeat, for example, may need to be put into proper accurate repeat, although this service may be carried out by a converter. In practice, the industry has now become highly complex, using a wide range of production models that can result in variation within a large company as to when a particular step occurs, let alone any correlation of where a competitor is in the same process. However, there are overarching timings, largely because of the previous history, and this goes some way to explain why print and pattern (for fashion and interiors in particular) is generally designed between a year and eighteen months before it reaches the shops.

From a design point of view, this means you have to try to work out what print the customer will look for at a particular time in the future. In many cases, professional designers get help with this. Trend books or websites may be made available by employers, and it is fairly common for a company's theme for a particular season to be decided prior to the prints being produced for it. In this case the designer is likely to have a fairly defined brief to work to. Most agencies and freelance studios do their own trends for their design teams - this can be quite formal, with clear resultant projects, or more informal, with the designers themselves having input to the process. Some employers or agencies may give their designers quite a lot (or even all) of the responsibility for coming up with the trends or inspiration for the print and pattern, so it is a valuable skill to have when looking for a job.

Above:
A spread from Dutch studio Amsterstampa's Stamp Stack trend book, designed by Frans Verschuren, Stefan Jans and Alex Russell.

Creating trends

Creating your own trends can appear a bit daunting at first; the notion that you will have any idea about what people will want pattern to look like in the future can seem faintly ridiculous. It is important to remember a few points here. Firstly, to remember that the word 'forecast' can be misleading here. All you are doing is presenting some design ideas with some supporting evidence to suggest why they might be relevant in the future. The evidence is there to give other people (and yourself) confidence to go with what you've suggested.

To massively over-simply the process, most trends do one of two things: Some seek to identify something that hasn't really been identified before. These tend to be based around a particular concept or idea. An example of this might start with an awareness that (largely because of online access) an ever-increasing number of people are working from home. How home-workers choose to decorate the space they work in, and what they might want to wear, could be developed as trends. The other type of trend suggests changing something that is already there, often by putting it with something else that it hasn't been combined with before, or by changing its context. This could involve taking a traditional pattern from the past, for example, and reworking it in new colours with digital technology.

Trend content

From a print point of view, most trends require four features: Firstly, a name and a paragraph that explains the trend and highlights its key attributes (it is almost impossible to make this too flowery or pretentious). Secondly, some images from any aspect of visual culture that serve as inspirational examples. Fairly commonly, it may be the combination of these images that inspires the trend, not how they work individually. Next is a colour palette. This is normally reflective of the colours in the inspirational images, and it is quite normal for each colour to be named to complement the title of the trend. These are also likely to include Pantone® or other colour matching system references. Finally, there are the print trends themselves – a series of designs that demonstrate how the trend could look if developed into a collection. It is standard practice for these to include illustrations on products; some may even include fabric samples (or samples on other appropriate surfaces). These are intended to show other designers how they might work with the trend, rather than be finished designs in themselves. The whole thing is normally presented in a way that picks up on the style of the trend, ideally enhancing the overall concept rather than intruding into its presentation.

External influences

Events or occurrences outside the creative industries may also have an impact on printed textile design. While these may seem very far removed from a designer sitting in a studio making a choice about what shade of red to use in a geometric pattern, world issues that appear at first unrelated to print design can cause shifts in taste or buying choices that may find their way through to influence practice in time. Being aware of these external influences and able to suggest how they might affect your employer's or client's needs is another valuable skill with which to arm yourself for a career.

Social change

How people live their lives has a big impact on the products they choose to buy, whether consciously or not. What people wear or use to decorate their homes makes a highly significant statement about themselves, and companies that use print and pattern are generally trying to figure out specific ways they can tap into this need for self-expression.

As people spend an increasing amount of their lives on the web, for example, social networking and working, forecasters will be trying to work out what impact this will have on what they consume. If shopping online, for instance, are people likely to make different decisions about buying patterned or printed product than if they were buying from a shop? It is important to understand that these changes may only affect small percentages of the population; no one is trying to say the whole world will follow the trend. Provided that the trend is present in a number felt to be significant enough to be considered a market (however niche), some businesses will be interested in trying to sell to them, and potentially in using the services of print and pattern designers to decorate their product.

Right:
Films with flamboyant art direction or styling, such as Sofia Coppola's *Marie Antoinette*, may prove influential as a source of trends.

Economic change

In times of austerity, people will buy fewer non-essentials; in some parts of the world, people can't buy them at all. In times of recession, a lot of design tends to look to escape, dipping into fantasy or (more commonly) times in the past seen as being more comfortable. Designers may be asked to rework historical designs, or the designs may simply be used as they were before.

Some companies will take a different route however, and try to encourage people to part with their money by looking to the future. This might involve experimenting with new visual ideas or emerging technologies.

World events and cultural occasions

Significant global events can also influence design. A major sporting event such as the World Cup or the Olympics is unlikely to cause large numbers of designers to start drawing footballs or running tracks to use in pattern. They might, however, look to the country hosting a future event for inspiration, aware that at a particular point in a couple of years, a lot of people will be thinking about that place.

Cultural occasions can affect what people might look at as well. The anniversary of a historical event that has a particular style associated with it could mean an upsurge of interest in that style. A film that has very strong art direction or a major international exhibition could also trigger a new trend. The number of people who have a significant impact on trends for print and pattern and the industries that use them is small, and many of them lead very similar lives, often visiting the same shops or galleries while they are in a particular city for a trade fair or fashion week, for example, with ideas from their expeditions later manifesting themselves as full-blown forecasts.

Above:
The work of designer Joasia Staszek is influenced by trends in the creative industries beyond textiles, including art direction and illustration.

Illustration, identity and art direction

Printed textile designers create pattern or imagery that is then applied to a product.

There are two main reasons it is invaluable to be able to illustrate how your designs would look when actually printed onto something. Firstly, it helps you to design better – it is always much easier to make decisions about whether a design will function in end-use if you can create a simulation of this to look at. In other words, you are able to satisfy yourself that the design will work, and able to adjust the design accordingly if you think it doesn't. Secondly, it is a powerful tool in convincing others of its value. Trying to explain in words how your design would look on a garment can be a lot more complex than just showing someone an illustration.

Print also has a part to play in the way products are sold. Companies may use printed textile practitioners to work with their identity, producing designs that feature their brand or logo. Pattern and print may also feature in styling and art direction, playing a part in visual merchandising or marketing.

The design world is a very competitive one, and faced with two similarly experienced candidates at interview, if one has the ability to illustrate their designs and show how they could be used in branding or point-of-sale, it is not hard to predict who a potential employer might recruit.

Right:
Carmen Wood created this illustration using the displace filter in Adobe Photoshop to combine one of her designs and a photo featuring a plain garment.

Illustration

Broadly speaking, there are two ways you can illustrate your print designs. The first way is to use a realistic drawing, photograph or other image of the product. While this will stop short of having to be a detailed technical diagram, it will give a fairly accurate depiction of the product, generally in a clean, clear format. The other method is to take a more stylized, artistic approach and show the design on a product in a way that still indicates end-use, but also evokes the mood or concept behind the design.

Above:
Seeing this wallpaper design by Dan Funderburgh in an interior setting gives a clear idea of its scale.

Ultimately, this is about visual communication and ways you can use it to instil confidence in your audience that your work fits the bill. There are parallels here with the way that you present your work overall. Perhaps the most important thing to keep in the back of your mind is this: imagine someone is looking at your folio without your actually being there. You are happy with the quality of the print designs, but want the viewer to see how your designs could work for them. A visualization or two for each design is likely go a long way in doing just that.

Illustration resources

To get started with being able to visualize your printed textiles design in interiors or on garments or other products, it is helpful to approach illustration from two different angles. The first thing to do is to start a library of other illustrators or designers. These might not show print or pattern; they might just be in a style you like or use a technique you want to try. Put another way, this is about style, rather than content. Try to make this library as easy to navigate as you can – it could be a physical thing you build up in a sketchbook, or something online such as a blog with links to interesting sites or images. The other approach is related to this, but deals with the products or settings rather than how they are depicted. Looking in as many places as you can, and including your own drawings or photographs, build up a collection of images of products that you think might be useful to contextualize you designs. If you are working with pattern for interiors, this could be drawings from architectural images, or your own photos of textile-covered furniture. People doing print for fashion could build up a collection of garment photographs, or draw from fashion shoots in magazines.

In either case, it is very important to respond to this collection of images. Work on your own experiments, practising in a range of media, using the libraries of style and content to work from.

98   **Chapter three: Context & communication**
The bigger picture ≪ | **Illustration, identity and art direction** | ≫ Chapter summary

Right:
This illustration by Claire Roberts is an example of a flat.

Diagrammatic illustration

For the purposes of this book, diagrammatic illustration is visualizing how a print or pattern might look in end-use in a simple, effective way. The image isn't trying to do anything other than give an example of end-use. The illustration will be reasonably realistic in terms of scale, but need not show a great deal of detail.

A good way of learning how to work this way is to work from garments or products you own. Take a few basic measurements from the object and scale them down to mark out a few key points on a piece of paper. Use these to draw the outline of the product, before adding construction details such as seams, stitches or any other fastenings. Designers often sketch these in pencil, inking them in when they are happy with all the proportions. Using different weights of line can significantly improve the look of your illustrations – try having the outlines wider, all important other construction in a medium line and detail such as stitching in a narrower weight. There are some particular digital techniques or media that particularly lend themselves to working in this way. Adobe® Illustrator® or other vector-based software packages are very commonly used for drawing garment flats (the fashion term for such an illustration).

There are a range of ways you can apply pattern to the illustration. You could do it digitally, via a scan if your product drawing is drawn by hand. You could draw the pattern directly onto the image, maybe photocopying it a few times first so you can try different things in the same end-use. Another approach is to get the product illustration copied onto acetate and lay it over the pattern. Remember that the pattern should be at the correct scale for the product (see the Author Tip).

'Illustration in its many forms has become more visible in everything from editorial, design and fashion publicity, to advertising, music, television and graphics.'

Angus Hyland

Above:
Print and pattern can also be illustrated in a more stylized manner. This may give less information about the product, but provides a more evocative, contextualized result.

Stylized illustration

A stylized illustration takes a more artistic approach than a diagrammatic one. The product it shows is more likely to be placed in some kind of context – an interior setting say, or someone wearing the garment. It can also be created in a way that helps to evoke the mood or concept behind the design, using a similar colour palette to the print design, for example, or placing the product in a scene that reflects one of the inspiration sources.

To practise this type of illustration, approach it from two angles. Firstly, look at the way other illustrators have done it, and try working in their style. Don't worry if this seem derivative at first; working from different sources, and as your confidence grows, so will your own style emerge. Secondly, try tracing the product you want to work with from photographs, either using conventional tracing paper or by working over the top of the photo digitally. Don't be put off if some people seem appalled by this – a surprising number of professional designers and illustrators use tracing as part of their working process. Mix elements from different photos together to get a more individual result, or draw some parts freehand. In time, this will help develop the proportion of your illustrations and you should find you can use the original photo just to reference rather than to trace from.

Realistically, print designers may find that investing time in learning how to do diagrammatic illustration may be of more benefit, not least because they are generally quicker to do and (crucially) of more help during the actual design process. However, if you need to explain the concept behind a collection, say, or are looking to broaden your skills base, stylized illustration can be a worthwhile area to explore.

> **AUTHOR TIP**
> **GETTING THE SCALE RIGHT**
>
> However you choose to illustrate your pattern in end-use, it is important to get a couple of things right. First, the scale – if your design is intended to be (say) 30cm high, it should be shown on the product at the correct size. The easiest way to get this right is to measure the size of an actual product and then work out roughly how big the design would be on it. For example, if your 30cm high design was going on a t-shirt, you could measure one of your own t-shirts. If this was 60cm high, then your print would be half the height of the t-shirt – the height of the t-shirt.

Branding

Branding is a company's attempt to do two things. Firstly to endear itself to its customers, often by trying to convince them that its products will satisfy their aspirations, and secondly to set themselves apart from their competitors, emphasizing characteristics of value or quality, for instance.

Some printed textile designers may find themselves working for a company that uses print as a central part of the branding process. This is particularly common in fashion, especially in the casual or jeans wear sectors. Practitioners are likely to not only find themselves using logos or other branded elements of text, but designing to visually communicate a philosophy that the company has developed to establish its identity. In some instances, the boundaries between graphics and printed textile design can appear very hazy – indeed a very large proportion of print or pattern design jobs in the fashion sector are advertised as posts for graphic designers. This should in no way put you off applying.

'You now have to decide what "image" you want for your brand. Image means personality. Products, like people, have personalities, and they can make or break them in the market place.'

David Ogilvy

Styling and content creation

As the boundaries between the traditional art and design disciplines become increasing blurred in the twenty-first century (due in large part to the increasing use of digital technology), it is important for printed textile designers to have an awareness of some of the new fields that they may find themselves working in.

A stylist creates a visual interpretation of a product or range. They might work for a fashion designer, helping to create the overall look of a show by producing its presentation, including choosing models, footwear, accessories and make-up styles. Stylists also work for magazines, putting merchandise together and deciding on locations, or with advertisers, helping to show off a client's products to their best advantage in a photo shoot. They generally work with photographers and often come from a fashion or textiles background. Perhaps surprisingly, they have been used by the furnishing industry for longer than fashion.

The role of art director is one of creative vision and leadership. The art direction of a photo shoot would not involve taking the photos, styling or booking the models or finding the location, for example, but it would involve coming up with the overall concept and making sure everyone involved produced results that successfully communicated that concept.

In recent years, pattern has been used not just to decorate products, but to market, advertise or visually merchandise them. This has led to a small but significant number of print and pattern designers working within art direction projects. In addition to this, some parts of the industry take a holistic view of the design and marketing process, seeing the visual content (including the print design) within them as being part of an over-arching art direction concept.

Right:
This design by
Maya Wild gives the
Adidas logo a
contemporary,
playful feel.

Chapter summary

In the competitive world of the textile industry, printed textile designers can place themselves at a considerable advantage if they can contextualize their work. This needs to reflect two things. Firstly, that they have an understanding of how the world around them can influence design and how to translate these influences into their work. Secondly, they understand what industry wants of them.

How a designer does this is essentially a process of visual communication. Although print design skills should be at the heart of your repertoire, being able to show you can present your work in context is very useful.

Printed textile designers are always designing for the future. Although a practitioner may find that the brief they are given contains the necessary details to ensure their work is right for its future customer, having a greater contextual awareness of how trends work, and being able to create your own, not only helps the design process but adds to your employability.

However you work, having a clear understanding of the contexts within which you operate and how to clearly communicate this will go a long way to giving your career some momentum.

Questions in summary

1. What part do trends play in printed textile design and the wider industry?
2. How might a printed textile designer work for fashion, furnishings and giftware/stationery outcomes?
3. What role does market research play in the design process?
4. What impact might social, economic or other global issues have on printed textile design?
5. What methods can a printed textile designer use to visually communicate their ideas?
6. How might a client's branding or identity become part of the print and pattern design process?

Style & content

Printed textile designs can be seen as having two main attributes: style and content. The style of a design is the way it looks or the form it takes. This might evoke a particular quality – delicate, say, or sophisticated.

Content is the imagery that a print or pattern design uses. This can be recognizable things – representations of flowers, for example, or birds. The content may also be abstract, perhaps using traditional pattern elements such as spots, or deriving new shapes from digital image manipulation. Very often the content is the first thing a client will mention when they are describing the type of design they want.

It is important to have an understanding of the different ingredients used to create designs. Colour as ever has a large part to play in this, and forms a crucial part in the style and season of a print. Furthermore, doing colourways (versions of the same design that use different colours) is a vital skill for printed textile designers to have. You may also be called on to create co-ordinates – groups of two or more patterns designed to work together.

The long, rich history of print and pattern is inextricably linked to its practice today. Printed textile practitioners are regularly asked to update or rework existing designs, and as a result of this have a working knowledge of a wide range of decorative looks or forms. Depending on the brief, printed textile designers need to be able to find the right balance of drawing on the past and looking to the future.

Design categories

Designs for printed textiles are often categorized by their content. This category is likely to be the a key word used to describe a particular print or pattern. Despite the fact that the definitions can be quite fluid and that not all terms are in use by all practitioners, they provide a useful way of introducing much of the key content of printed textiles. This section will look at six main groups that can be used to define different types of print and pattern. Not every pattern can be described by the terms, and some may feature combinations of content that means they straddle the different categories, but they do provide a useful way to introduce much of the subject matter that print designers have to work with.

The six groups are florals, geometrics, graphic designs, conversationals, historic styles and geographic styles. The exact taxonomy may vary in name and structure over different markets and sectors of the industry; if you are working with someone from another country, many of the terms do not literally translate to other languages (although the elements within them could be derived from all over the globe). None the less, these terms do cover most of the imagery used in print and pattern and given an idea of the extraordinary range of style and content you may be required to employ.

Florals

The imagery most commonly used in printed textile design is based on flowers. Designs with floral content are so ubiquitous that they can be subdivided into any number of different styles or categories. Botanicals, for example, may be used to describe very accurately painted florals (because they look like botanical illustrations). They can be associated with particular historical looks, cultures or designer companies. Florals that draw on William Morris's designs, for example, are likely to have a late Victorian or Arts and Crafts style. On the other hand, images of cherry blossoms or chrysanthemums are sometimes used to give a Japanese feel as both flowers are associated with that culture. By the same token, the term Liberty floral or print can refer to any multi-directional, small-scale floral in the style of the London-based company. Florals may include other elements from plants, such as leaves or stems, or be mixed with geometric or conversational motifs. Such designs can be very realistic – digital printing allows photographs of flowers to be used, for example – or be highly abstract.

The popularity of florals

There are a number of reasons for their popularity. People are very familiar with their use, as they have been a part of print and pattern for a very long time. Flowers feature in designs from almost every part of the globe, and occur prominently in the historic Indian designs, for instance, that have had such an influence on textile prints all over the world. Some have argued that there is a link between the huge amounts of floral fabric printed during the Industrial Revolution and the rapidly increasing urban population at that time – as people had less contact with the countryside, buying printed flower designs became a way of keeping in touch with the natural world.

'There is nothing you can see that is not a flower.'

Matsuo Bashō

The significance of florals

From a semiotic standpoint, flowers can be seen as signifying the beauty of nature. Indeed, although it is not commonly referenced by designers, there is a whole folklore language of flowers. This may occasionally have an impact in a negative way. Lilies, for instance, may be associated with death and (admittedly few) companies can be reluctant to use designs that feature them. Flowers feature heavily in most products that printed textile designers create work for, with the exception of men's and boy's fashion, where their use tends to be limited. The stereotypical view of florals is that they can be interpreted as feminine; whether there is any link between the widespread use of flowers in textile design and a very high percentage of practitioners being women is open to discussion.

Designing florals

For the designer, florals are a highly versatile vehicle for expressing almost any style or design theme, capable of looking subtle and delicate or brash and bold. A skilled practitioner can make a design featuring flowers look several centuries old or very contemporary. In a discipline where colour plays such a big part, they provide visual content that can feature almost any hue, tone or saturation whilst still maintaining a semblance of realism. If you don't have a floral collection in your portfolio and you are looking to broaden its range, a collection of designs that prominently feature flowers should be your priority.

Geometrics and abstract patterns

Geometrics and abstracts are non-representational designs – pure pattern that doesn't look like any actual thing. The terms are fairly interchangeable, although in some cases, the word geometric is used to describe designs with quite an ordered, clean look, whereas abstract may refer to something looser or more flowing. The designs can be developed from figurative imagery, derived from experimenting with simple shapes or obtained by any number of other methods. Like florals, they have been associated with printed textile design for its entire history. Long before Western artists began painting abstract pictures, Western designers were working with abstract content, often derived from sources such as Islamic decorative arts that themselves have a long and rich heritage of pattern. It is rare to find ornament in any culture that does not make at least some use of abstract or geometric content.

Geometrics and abstracts in context

Certain geometric patterns can have very particular meanings, which can become ignored or distorted when appropriated elsewhere. Prior to the Second World War, the swastika symbol was widely found in pattern all over the world, and is still in common use in a number of Eastern religions. However, its adoption by the Nazi Party in 1920, and the subsequent association of the symbol with Nazism meant that it is far too emotive an element to be included in any Western design. Indeed, its use is illegal in some European countries, unless employed as a religious symbol.

The source of some geometric staples is quite clear; plaid and herringbone designs, for example, both come from weaving structures. Others may have evolved in such as way that their roots are less obvious. Arabesque patterns are probably most influenced by Islamic art, but the complex intertwined design elements they feature can also be traced back to Greek or Roman decorative art.

Above:
Very simple geometric elements such as spots can be used in more complex designs.

Types of geometrics

The most common examples of geometrics are probably stripes, spots (or dots) and checks (or plaids), although the last of these are less common for print designers to work with, being more the preserve of weave. These three are used so widely, they tend to be referred to directly – in other words, a spot will be called a spot, rather than a geometric. These basic design structures, so simple at first glance, are often overlooked by students of printed textiles. Even the most cursory market research will reveal how commonly they are used by industry; if you don't have any in your portfolio, it would be well worth adding a few.

Creating geometric and abstract designs

Don't be fooled into thinking that designs that appear very simple can be quickly and thoughtlessly churned out. Although the final design itself may not take long to create, particularly when working digitally, it is likely to require just as much zdeliberation and reflection as a far more complex design. In fact, the ability to create good stripe or spot patterns, operating with a small palette and what appears to be the most uncomplicated of structures, is probably one of the fundamental measures of a print and pattern designer's ability. Working only with colour and proportion, with no imagery or other content to hide behind, can quickly become something of an obsession (in a good way). Doubters of a simple geometric's ability to be distinctive need look no further than a Burberry check or a Paul Smith stripe; that working with apparently simple abstract structures is an intellectual activity is borne out in fine art by Bridget Riley's stripes or Gerhard Richter's colour chart paintings and in the designs of the large number of anonymous textile designers who do similar work.

Textured designs

Another fairly common geometric or abstract is a textured design. The print is made up of an all-over surface effect, often obtained by some form of mark making or other non-representational use of traditional painting or drawing media. In production, this is often achieved by using two or more very similar colours; if the colours are the same hue but vary only in how light or dark they are, this may be referred to as tone on tone. The subtle effect this achieves is particularly common in furnishing and home / interior design. When creating such a design, the texture itself may be relatively easy to achieve; putting it into repeat can be much harder.

Geometric motifs

Many geometric motifs are described using words that sound quite poetic to an outsider, but refer to something very specific to a printed textile designer; this is in contrast to the word 'geometric', which sounds as if it might refer to something rigidly mathematical in design. Verimicular, trefoils, foulards and cartouches all have historical associations with different types of abstract pattern, and although they may not be as widely used now as they were in the past, the designs they describe can be a valuable reference point for contemporary designers.

'I think certain types of processes don't allow for any variation. If you have to be part of that process, all you can do is transform – or perhaps distort – yourself through that persistent repetition, and make that process a part of your own personality.'

Haruki Murakami

Graphic designs

Graphic designs often feature text or branding, sometimes with accompanying imagery of some sort. They tend to be placement designs (they are very common on t-shirts, for instance) and are by far the most commonly seen in the fashion sector, especially in the sport, swim, street and jeanswear areas. Indeed, printed textile designers are normally referred to as graphic designers within the fashion industry – something to bear in mind when job hunting.

Graphics in textile design

Working with graphic designs can prove more complex than it may at first appear. Drawing too heavily on another company's logo could result in legal action, as most brands are fiercely protective of their corporate identity. Print designers may however find that they are asked to use particular logos or brands as inspiration. The skilled practitioner can come up with something new and fictitious that captures the flavour of the source material in an original way. Some of these styles have become so ubiquitous, it becomes impossible to associate them with a single brand. The number of fashion and sportswear brands that dip into an American Collegiate look, for example, are legion.

Working with text

Using text can also present problems. Firstly, in most cases, using a particular font in a commercial design requires it to be licensed for that use. If you are working for a particular company, they will almost certainly have the licence for any fonts they use in their visual identity, and therefore this won't be an issue. However, if you are working freelance and do a design to go on sale that features a particular font, by the letter of the law, the buyer would have to purchase their own licence to use the font (as well as buying the design off you).

The most obvious way round this is to design your own font, possibly using an existing one as a starting point. If this seems a bit complex, remember you can just 'draw' your own letters, or use software to adapt existing ones (this is particularly easy with vector-based programs such as Adobe® Illustrator®).

The second issue with using text can come if you use words written in other languages or alphabets. If you don't know what the characters say, you run the risk that they might be offensive or inappropriate to a native speaker. Ideally, you should check the meaning before you sign the design off.

Similar concerns may come into play if you use images of fictional characters. The right to use cartoon characters, for example, will normally be held by the production company that makes the cartoon. Unless you have express permission from them, you should steer clear of such imagery.

‘Graphic design is the paradise of individuality, eccentricity, heresy, abnormality, hobbies and humours.’

George Santayana

Conversationals

Conversationals are representational designs that are not florals. In other words, they contain imagery that depicts actual objects or things other than flowers. The term is not universally used – they may also be known as novelty or object prints, or be further categorized by their content. The content of a conversational is crucial to its success and particular subject matter may be at the mercy of fashions to a far greater degree than florals or geometrics. Some conversationals remain in fashion, but polarise opinion. Animal skin prints (designs that appear to be zebra, leopard or snake skin, for example) can be seen as completely kitsch or highly sophisticated, depending on the stance of the viewer (and the quality of the design). However, they crop up in one form or another a lot and there is no harm is being versed in using them.

Using conversationals

Some conversational design groups have grown out of functional use into something more playful. A number of designers have used camouflage as a starting point, sometimes subverting it with bright colours or inserting imagery or text into it. Indeed, in some quarters, an all-over multidirectional repeat in fairly muted colours has become known as a camo or camouflage print.

Some conversationals are fairly immune to the vagaries of trends. Birds, in particular, are used fairly frequently, as are butterflies, although even these tend to go through cycles of being in vogue. Conversationals may also be associated with particular events or, say, holidays in the calendar.

Conversationals are probably at their most common in the giftware and stationery sector, possibly because designers in this area may come from an illustration or graphics background (where the use of narrative is more usual) or simply because customers are likely to be much more adventurous with the imagery they wrap a present in (say) than that which they choose to wear or cover their furniture with. In fashion, children's wear is probably the most common product to feature conversationals.

Historic styles

A historic style is one that draws on the decorative elements associated with a particular period or art or design movement. This is normally done to deliberately link a design to a specific (or specifically imagined) point in the past. A design might be created digitally and printed using the most advanced printing methods onto a fabric that is at the cutting edge of technical development, but if it references an eighteenth-century French wallpaper design, it will appear to have a heritage that to some eyes makes it more authentic or dependable a choice than a very contemporary design. Although historic styles are used in all areas of printed textile design, they are probably more common in furnishing designs than fashion. Furthermore, where they are used in fashion, they are likely to reference a more recent moment in the past.

Revisiting the past

As with the other categories of printed textile design, historic styles have a number of different names. Designs that are inspired by the more recent past tend to be termed retro rather than historic. A print that aimed to capture a 1960s or 1970s feel would normally be called retro, whereas a design that had been created to encapsulate the look of the 1860s would be historic. Equally, historical styles may be referred to by the look they draw on. In the 1920s and 30s, designers became increasingly influenced by then-recent developments in fine art, particularly cubism and constructivism, and much print and pattern of the time has a distinctly modernist look. Designs produced now that seek to re-create this look would be known as art deco rather than historical. Many other art movements of the last century were used by designers as inspiration.

Historic styles can themselves be based on earlier styles. At the heart of the Arts and Crafts style was a reaction against industrialization, and the practitioners such as William Morris who developed it looked back to a pre-industrial age, seeking inspiration from the decorative arts of the Middle Ages in particular. This also serves to illustrate a likely reason for the popularity of historic pattern – it can bring to mind a romanticized suggestion of the past, suggesting, for example a simpler, better way of life.

Archive and vintage designs

Industry does not always have to trouble practitioners to create new designs in an old style. A number of companies specialize in selling archive print and pattern. In many cases, these designs are then used exactly as they are, although some adaptations may be made to them. Colours may be updated, for example, or if the entire repeat is not visible, designers will re-create it. The archival designs may come in a number of different forms. Many print companies of the nineteenth century, for example, had pattern books that they used as a catalogue of the designs they had manufactured. These have page after page of designs, generally either as fabric swatches or gouache paintings, often packed together so that 20 or 30 patterns are shown on a spread. The designs in such sources are sold or licensed to companies to use. In many cases, when these designs go on sale, they are marketed using their heritage as the focus of their appeal. Some companies that have been established for a long time have their own archives to draw on. This has been fairly common practice in furnishing print for some time, but is also seen in fashion.

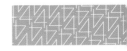

Above:
This design updates an old baroque pattern with hand-drawn effects.

Geographic styles

Geographic is a catch-all term used to describe print and pattern designs that are inspired by a particular culture, and generally one associated with a particular place. A number of other names may be used to describe this group (such as folk or ethnic designs), and it is probably more common for the designs to be referred to by the culture or location that inspired them.

There are an extraordinary range of geographic styles in printed textile design. For as long as there has been trade between countries and cultures, patterned textiles and other decorative objects have been bought and sold. Over the centuries, people have been used to seeing designs from all over the world; pattern has always featured in the global marketplace and been a feature of international trade. Some motifs used in designs can be traced back hundreds or even thousands of years. Even more recent additions to the canon have often undergone complex evolution, in part influenced by changes in trade or fashion.

Vintage designs for fashion

Some companies or studios specialize in selling vintage garments or accessories so that the print on them can be used for new clothing. Some studios that formerly only carried original work in their portfolios now have vintage stock to sell to their clients. Indeed, some printed textiles designers would include looking for old fabrics or garments in their research process, scouring charity or junk shops for inspiration. Selling on garments does raise issues of ownership – if you sell on a vintage design for someone else to use, you are in theory selling the copyright that the company that made it owns. Specialists in this area will look for items that are old enough for their copyright to have expired. They may also look for clothing made by brands or manufacturers that no longer exist.

Well-travelled pattern

The paisley motif can be seen in both Indian and Persian culture and is so old its exact inspiration has been lost. Some sources suggest it is derived from the shape of a mango, others from a stylized flower; most are agreed that it is likely to have been inspired at least in part by plant forms. The pattern was introduced to Europe in the seventeenth and eighteenth centuries from India, and became particularly associated with exquisite hand-woven cashmere shawls that could take up to five years to make. Needless to say, these were wildly expensive and European textile companies looked to capitalize on the style's desirability by mass producing cloth featuring the pattern. One of the centres of this production was the Scottish town of Paisley, which gave its name to the design style in the West.

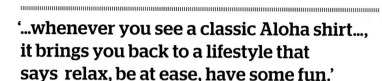
'...whenever you see a classic Aloha shirt...,
it brings you back to a lifestyle that
says relax, be at ease, have some fun.'

Dale Hope

Opposite:
Use of bold colours
and the hibiscus
flower gives this
geographic design
a Hawaiian style.

Western adaptation of Eastern pattern

The notion of a style having its roots in one
geographic location, and then being filtered
through another, is widespread. Another example
of it is Chinoiserie. Demand for the beautiful
ornamentation of Chinese decorative arts grew
steadily following Marco Polo's travels in the late
thirteenth century. By the seventeenth century,
they were fairly widely available throughout
Europe, although they remained highly prized
and expensive. By the mid-eighteenth century,
manufacturers were creating their own goods
that drew heavily on Chinese style. These became
very fashionable and the style became known
as Chinoiserie (*Chinois* is French for Chinese).

The style has remained a staple of printed
textile design (particularly for interiors) ever since.
Whilst it was (and remains) obviously influenced
by Chinese decorative arts, it is an interpretation
of their work, fed through the eighteenth-century
eyes of the design studios of (say) French or British
manufacturers. The content is somewhat
formulaic – paper lanterns and pagodas feature
heavily – and is shorn of its original visual
vocabulary. The way they are depicted clearly
reflects Western pattern design of that period and
the term Chinoiserie has come to mean designs
that look like the eighteenth-century Europe
take on Chinese applied arts, rather than designs
directly derived from the visual culture of China.

The significance of geographic styles

Just as florals could be seen as providing a
sense of escape from the built environment
to a more bucolic world, so the geographic can
provide imaginary passage to other lands or more
exotic cultures. As already noted with Chinoiserie,
the surface pattern applied to a product could be
used to evoke a culture too distant to visit or
whose goods would be too expensive for most
people to own. Another example of this can be
seen on summer or swim wear that makes use
of the imagery associated with Aloha (Hawaiian)
shirts, using the motifs to create a relaxed, surf feel.

From a cultural theory standpoint, the use of
pattern from other cultures may raise issues. In a
similar way to designers exercising caution with
the use of text or alphabets in different languages
or the use of some geometric symbols, so can the
use of pattern sometimes need to be treated with
care. A motif might have religious significance,
for example, and its use on a consumer product
might be seen as offensive to some people. It
can also be easy for designs to appear clichéd
if they draw on too-obvious reference points.
A more sophisticated approach can successfully
evoke a place's atmosphere without
appearing stereotypical.

Colourways and co-ordinates

Above:
A design for digital fabric printing depicted in its original colourway.

There are a number of key skills that printed textile designers need in addition to creating print and pattern. Practitioners may be asked to come up with alternative versions of designs, either in different colours or as a series of (generally simpler) variations of the original. This section will look at colourways and co-ordinates, and examine some of the issues designers have to think about if their patterns are to work on a number of products with different surfaces.

Defining colourways

A colourway is an alternative version of a design in different colours. In other words, everything about the design is exactly the same except the colour of each part of it. The total number of colours very rarely changes – if the original has six colours, so will all the colourways. In some cases, this involves keeping the tones about the same, so the areas that had the lightest colour in the original remain the lightest in the colourway, the darkest areas stay the darkest, and so on. However, sometimes the look of the original will be radically altered by using different tones, probably the most significant of which is the base or background colour (if the design has one). It should be noted that however different the colourway, this would not alter who owns the copyright. If you re-colour a design, it is still the same design in law.

Colourways are probably more common in the furnishing industry than in fashion or other sectors, but they can still be seen almost everywhere that there is pattern. In addition, fabrics for interiors may be offered in a wider range of different colourways than for fashion; at the high end of the market, they may even be available to order in unique colours for a specific customer. In some cases, a design may be available for years, with re-colourings every few years to keep in step with wider trends in colour.

DISCUSSION POINT
GETTING TO GRIPS WITH COLOURWAYS

Pick a design to work on that has a palette of about four or five colours.

Keeping the tones about the same in the first instance, work out a palette that is different in hue or saturation from the original – warm colours rather than cold, or bright shades instead of muted ones.

Working with a duplicate of the original, carefully replace all of each colour in turn. Remember that the total number of colours should be the same in the colourway as the original and that all the elements that were (say) red to start with should be end up (say) blue in the duplicate.

Now try doing another where the tone changes – you could make the lightest original colour the darkest in the colourway. Try to change the atmosphere or mood as much as you can.

Using colourways

The prosaic reason that a number of colourways for a design might be offered to the customer is simply that it increases the likelihood of that product being sold. If colour is the most important reason for a particular pattern to sell, having more than one colourway available increases the chances of it being bought. Furthermore, it is normally cheaper to buy and manufacture a design in (say) three colourways than it is to work with three separate designs. This is particularly noticeable at the printing stage – the set-up of the rotary screens is expensive from scratch, but once they have been made, any combination of colours can be run through them. As this applies to any print process (except digital printing), it is highly likely that this is why colourways evolved in the first place. This is also the reason that colourways almost invariably have the same number of colours as the original – they use exactly the same rollers, screen or blocks as the original.

Traditionally, painting out colourways was often the preserve of junior designers; copying existing designs in new colours being seen as an important part of their training. The choice of the colours would be likely to come from a more senior member of the studio. Digital technology has radically increased the speed with which colourways can be created and it is a key feature of all dedicated printed textiles design software packages (and perfectly possible in almost any visual editing program). However, being able to create good colourways remains a difficult skill to master and this is a prime example of computing technology making something quicker, not easier.

Left:
The same design is shown here in a different colourway.

Learning to work with colourways

As colourways are likely to play a part in the career of a printed textile designer, it is important that your portfolio demonstrates that you can do them. If you are working for a company, for example, you may be called on to show how one of your designs would look in a number of different colourways from a particular palette. If you are a freelance designer, it can help to sell a design if you can show how it would look in an Autumn/Winter colourway as opposed to a Spring/Summer one. In addition, it also goes some way to demonstrate you could comfortably work with either season if commissioned.

Colour and timescale

As the content of a print or pattern plays a part in defining its style, so colour is just as important in the final effect (if not more so). Colour cannot be separated from print and pattern and just as certain elements can be crucial in communicating a particular look, so can colour. Indeed, a motif that seems to define a particular look can have its meaning completely altered by changing its colours. You could take almost any design from any point in time, and if you changed its colours to bright yellows, oranges, pinks, purples and lime greens it would look like a late 1960s psychedelic design.

A palette doesn't have to be particularly big to evoke a particular style – even a couple of colours can immediately call to mind certain moments in design history. The use of jade green and fuchsia pink are likely to bring the 1980s flooding into any design, for example. Printed textile designers can harness this extraordinary power colour has to their advantage, carefully selecting colours to ensure that the final design can do everything possible to convey the style required of it.

Researching colour

Linking the colour in a design to a particular moment in history involves two main steps – finding the palette and then successfully using it. The process of finding the colours is essentially research, but needs to be very objective and focused. If the brief asks you to work in a 1950s style, you might look for some images of decorative objects, interiors or other design from that time. If they exist and you can access them, looking at book or magazine illustrations for the period in question can be really helpful. It is important that your own personal taste doesn't get in the way of this – you may find an example of colour use that (subjectively) you really like, but if it isn't capable of conjuring the response that the brief requires, you shouldn't use it. The problem can be compounded if you have been asked to work with a very limited number of colours.

The next step is to decide which of the colours in your research you are going to use. This can only be done by physically trying out the colours, paying particular attention to the proportions they are used in. It is also important to match the colours as accurately as possible. Pulling (say) five colours out of five different images and assuming that they will work together is unlikely to work. Prior to computers, designers often spent some time mixing paint up to match the colour they wanted, possibly trying them out in simple stripes of colour, using the width of the stripes to get the proportions right. Digital technology can significantly speed this process up, allowing you to eye-drop colour straight out of a scan (say) and immediately fill all the relevant parts of a design with it. The speed at which this is possible can be very seductive; objectively judging that the colours are right for the job they are supposed to do remains where the skill lies.

Historic or geographical use of colour in pattern is often linked to the technology that would have been used to print the designs. The blues and browns associated with traditional Indonesian batiks would form a vital part of the colour palette if a brief asked you to create designs in that style. The dyers of the original fabrics had a limited range of natural colours at their disposal – the palette that has become associated with them stems from these limits.

Creating vintage colour

Whilst almost any colour palette can be made to look older by some combination of fading, desaturation or mixing it towards sepia, you should not assume that the past was automatically more muted. Mention has already been made of the Mauve decade in chapter one; some of the interiors that typify the Belle Epoque at the end of the nineteenth century contain remarkably strident mixes of bright colour and clashing pattern.

Particularly when designing for fashion, don't forget the role that seasonal colour plays in all this. If you are designing for Spring/Summer, but your research is suggesting you use very dark, cold colours, you may need to cast the net a bit wider.

Co-ordinates

A co-ordinate is a design that is intended to be used with a different print or pattern. A traditional example of this could be a wallpaper border, meant to run at (say) dado rail height around a room, with different co-ordinating wallpapers above and below.

Designs that have been created to co-ordinate generally do so in two ways. Firstly (and most obviously), they will use the same colour palette. They might not all contain the same number of colours though – a fairly complex design with (say) eight colours might have a co-ordinate that features two of them in a simple stripe. Secondly, it is quite likely that the co-ordinates could feature one or more elements of the (normally more complex) main design. A floral pattern that featured ten different flowers arranged in repeat might have a co-ordinate with just one of the same flowers, perhaps at a smaller scale and arranged in a different repeat structure.

Right:
Design company
People will always
need Plates'
distinctive style
ensures that the
different designs
in their tablewear
co-ordinate.

Co-ordinates in use

Co-ordinates tend to be more commonly
found in furnishing or homeware than in
fashion. Customers buying bedding, for instance,
might find that a duvet cover has one design
and the pillow cases that come with it have
a separate, but co-ordinating design on them.
As already suggested, traditional wallpapers
are often designed with a border or to go with
another paper.

In fashion, it is relatively rare for co-ordinating
print designs to be used in the same garment, but
more common in designs for a range of garments.
One item of clothing might feature an all-over
repeat; another might have a placement printing
using a single motif from the first. Curiously,
design studios who show their collection as
blanks quite often combine co-ordinating prints
in them. Co-ordinates tend to be used in a similar
way in giftware or stationery. A single design
might be adapted a number of different ways
to suit a range of products.

'That's something I learned
in art school... my professor
emphasized the responsibility
that designers and illustrators
have towards the people they
create things for.'

Eric Carle

Right:
Klaus Haapaniemi's design is part of a larger range of co-ordinating crockery for Iittala.

Same design, different surface

Just as a number of different designs can be created to work together as co-ordinates, so can one design be used on a variety of different surfaces or products. It could be that the design is used with no changes at all; the fabric could be printed first, for example, and then made into two different styles of top. Occasionally a design could have its scale altered, although such a change would require a separate set of (say) rotary screens and might be termed a co-ordinate.

One important issue that printed textile designers need to be aware of is the effect that the weight or construction of the fabric may have on the colour in a design. A design printed with the exact same batch of dyestuff onto a silk chiffon and a silk velvet will look very different on the two fabrics, particularly in use. The colours on the chiffon will appear far paler than they will on the velvet; on the heavy fabric, the colour will be far deeper and may even have a metallic quality.

The construction of the fabric may also have a bearing. If the fabric is textured or woven from a coarse yarn, it will not show fine detail well; the uneven surface of the fabric will break up fine lines, for example. By contrast, a fine weave or knit will carry the design better, its smoother surface providing a more accurate translation of the design. It is interesting to note that digital fabric printing is actually dependent on some surface texture, however subtle this is. The way the tiny drops of dyestuff hit the surface of the fabric is made slightly unpredictable by the texture of the fabric surface. This helps with the optical mixing that makes a fixed number of printing colours provide a full spectrum.

If you are designing print or pattern for giftware or another end-use where the print is likely to be onto paper or another surface other than fabric, you can be fairly sure that the substrate will be selected to ensure that the printer will be able to get an pretty accurate colour match of your design. However, the palette may still be altered by the surface or there still may be limitations on the colours that the print process can provide.

Change and evolution

There are a number of professional design skills that can be difficult for students or new designers to acquire. One of these is the common requirement of being able to work with a broad range of colour, style and content; often this involves updating traditional designs. As a professional designer, you will be required to create work that may have little if any connection to your own personal taste or desire for self-expression. At first, this can seem difficult to grasp, but you should never forget that it is very often the print or pattern that sells the product; the person who buys it does so because of your skill in adding value to it.

If a brief does ask you to produce an innovative range of print designs, you should not assume that this means you cannot find inspiration in imagery from the past. Re-contextualizing or adapting historical pattern can result in ground-breaking new work. Explaining this may be made easier if its visual language references are established design elements. The past can also reveal valuable lessons about how innovation can come from technological advances.

Right:
The origins of paisley are unclear, although it is thought to be based on some natural form, possibly the mango.

Design adaptation

New designers are often surprised to discover how self-referential the industry is. Indeed, for many printed textile practitioners, one of the most fundamental skills is the ability to adapt existing designs. A common example of this involves taking a classic pattern and reworking it in a more contemporary style. In some cases, a particular designer may be used because their handwriting coincides with the look that the client wants, but more commonly the output is a more anonymous update of a theme that may date back centuries.

'Things alter for the worse spontaneously, if they be not altered for the better designedly.'

Francis Bacon

'**The successful textile designer seeks not to devise something never before imagined but to create a variation on… pre-existing themes.**'

Susan Mellor and Joost Elffers

Innovation

Of course, there are printed textile designers out there creating work that is new, innovative and original. However, if you don't have experience of the industry, you should be aware that a very substantial proportion of new designs are essentially recycled versions of old ones. The history of many of these design staples dates back to a time long before originality and self-expression were valued by artists and designers. This is not the place to judge whether this is a good thing or not, but for every attention-garnering contemporary design that breaks boundaries, there are an awful lot of highly commercially successful ones that draw heavily on the rich heritage of the past.

As with any project, the designer must answer the brief and many clients will assume that if you are offering your services, you can adapt almost anything to suit their needs. Because of this, if you are interested in working with a broad range of clients, it is a good idea to be able to work with most of the content and a number of the styles outlined in this chapter.

Certain patterns have become so ever-present that they are used in a large number of designs all the time; others dip in and out of fashion, resurfacing in a new guise as designers discover ways of re-working them. You should be aware that some motifs have particular connotations with people depending on their age or cultural background. Paisley, for example, may look unforgivably hippyish to some eyes, despite its use on bohemian 60s fashion being a single moment of the motif's long and illustrious history. It is also important to understand that particular styles of pattern can go in and out of fashion very quickly, but that this doesn't necessarily apply to every market or end-use.

Right:
A 60s retro style
design for
wallpaper.

Working in different styles

As a professional designer, it will do you no harm
at all to be able to work in a wide range of different
styles. Although it is possible that you could spend
your entire career designing for the same
company, and potentially it might be a company
with a very distinctive style that would be
unlikely to alter much, the likelihood is that even
if you do only ever work in one place, they will
change at least some of the content in their range.
In practice, it is far more likely that you will find
yourself working in a variety of styles; at the
very least it is an excellent idea to have a few in
your portfolio to demonstrate your adaptability
to potential employers or agents.

There are two things that are really important
to keep in mind when asked to design in a new
style. The first is that you will need to do some
effective research. In some cases, you might
be lucky enough to be provided with a few key
images as part of the brief, but it is much more
likely that you will just get a few words to start.
It can be very helpful to clarify a few details
with whoever has set the brief. For example,
if you are asked to design in a 1960s style, this
could be in the clean graphic style of Mary Quant
or a psychedelic, hippy look – the two are very
different. Getting the client to name a few key
designers or artists, or quickly e-mailing them
a few source images for confirmation can be
invaluable in starting on the right track. Being
clear of the style you are working with goes
hand-in-hand with finding imagery you can
work from.

Researching new styles

Obviously, where you look will depend on the
style you have been asked to work with. Given
a historical style, for example, you could look for
some images of key design or art from that period,
bookmarking or saving the ones that you think
best evoke the ambience you are after. Looking
at magazine images (including adverts) from the
time concerned can be really helpful, although
this is of course dependent on there being this
resource for the time you are looking at. Unless
specifically told otherwise, don't limit yourself
to looking at only printed textile design – other
design or decorative or applied arts may be just
as helpful. With some styles, you might need
to research architecture or art; all that matters is
that the image successfully conveys the character
of the style.

The Internet, and in particular resources such
as Google® Images, have made this a lot easier,
but you still may need to be quite discerning about
the search terms you use. As suggested on page 13,
most designers build up a fairly extensive library
of books and magazine to work from. However,
you should never underestimate the importance
of primary research, and you should aim to
develop your own design elements in the style
you have been asked to work in as soon as
possible. Remember that if you do use found
imagery in your designs, it is highly likely you
will break copyright law. It is therefore a good
idea to get into the habit of never using found
imagery as anything other than a reference
source unless you have been specifically asked
to do this by your client or employer, or can be
absolutely certain the images you use will not
breach copyright.

Right:
A traditional
damask design.

Using research to inform new styles

This leads to the second important thing to think about when working in a new style – use the research. Keep the key images you have found in front of you when you are working and regularly step back from the development or design you are working on to check that it captures the essence of what you are aiming for. This can be a particular concern if the style is new to you. In this situation, where you may feel quite unconfident with your ability to successfully work in that way, it can be easy (possibly even subconsciously) to use techniques or elements that might make you feel more comfortable with the design, but are actually tangential to it properly reflecting the style you've been asked to convey.

Working with either floral or conversational content normally involves honing the particular technique or media the brief's style requires alongside developing new images from the research material. This may involve working from life in the case of florals, refining the process until you feel ready to work on the final design or collection. Geometric designs may come as the result of doodling, experimentation with particular software or mathematical investigation. In any case, having images to refer to that demonstrate the style the brief asks of you is crucial to staying on track.

From historical to contemporary

Working with source material from the past need not be at the expense of innovation. Designs that appear contemporary may in fact be deeply rooted in history. Whilst you may re-work print or pattern from the past with the specific intent of keeping its period aesthetic, you could also radically change this by re-contextualizing the design in some way. This may involve a relatively minor change, or could include significant change, mixing in a wide range of different elements.

One of the staple styles of printed textile design is damask. The name normally refers to symmetrical designs, loosely based on plant forms, but generally abstracted into flowing graphic forms. As with many other patterns that have been around for centuries, the origins of the style have been lost in time, and it is likely that it came from several sources. Some argue that the symmetrical geometry of damask designs was thought to have been first introduced to the West as robes bought by Marco Polo on his travels. The name refers to Damascus, a major trading centre of the time. Others also cite Damascus, but as the origin of the fabrics – the area was a centre for the weaving industry from the early Middle Ages.

***

'The charm of history and its enigmatic lesson consist in the fact that, from age to age, nothing changes and yet everything is completely different.'

Aldous Huxley

Updating designs

Some of these damask designs retain the historic look, but others use colour or the addition of elements to appear more contemporary. They might feature strong differences in colour such as black and white, or use on-trend palettes, featuring metallics, for instance. Other designers add non-traditional imagery, achieving a more up-to-date look, but retaining some of the traditional form.

At the time of writing, the popularity of the style shows no signs of abating. Trying to work out which patterns of the present will come to be seen in the future as typical is difficult, but it doesn't require a huge leap of faith to suggest that a damask wallpaper will come to be seen as one of the key prints of the early part of this century. One possible explanation for the style's attractiveness to designers may be connected to the increasing use of digital technology. In almost any software, copying and mirroring a design element is very easy; damask-like designs can be built up quite quickly from relatively simple elements.

Initially, damask designs were woven, not printed. The fabric was very expensive and gradually much cheaper printed versions began to appear, both as fabric and on wallpaper. Initially these sought to mimic the style of the woven versions as closely as possible, in particular often featuring only two colours, generally quite close in colour and tone – one for the ground and one for the symmetrical forms. The design remained in fairly frequent use, mostly for furnishings, but normally retained its historic look. The first few years of the twenty-first century saw its popularity increase significantly, particularly as wallpaper.

Opposite:
William Morris's designs have had a profound influence on printed textiles, but reacted against industrial developments rather than using them to innovate.

Heritage and innovation

Printed textile design is not traditionally a high profile activity. The designers who are better known tend to be the ones who manufacture product as well, not the in-house or freelance practitioners. It is rare for a print designer to be credited on a product, for example, and innovation in print may be more associated with a particular brand or product rather than a named designer.

One of the significant changes in the practice since the turn of the millennium has been the ease with which it is possible to access sources of contemporary print and pattern. There are an increasing number of books devoted to showcasing the work of current practitioners, many of which suggest that interest in print and pattern has never been greater. These books are of huge benefit in allowing students and professionals alike to quickly get a survey of what is out there. This was possible previously, but required time and effort to go out and conduct market research – the dedicated books on printed textiles that were published tended to focus on historic or period design. The Internet also makes research into innovative design far easier. Even if it takes some digging about to find the good sites, blogs or portals, there's lots of constantly updated source material out there.

'Learning and innovation go hand in hand. The arrogance of success is to think that what you did yesterday will be sufficient for tomorrow.'

William Pollard

AUTHOR TIP
DESIGN ADAPTATION AND COPYRIGHT

Print and pattern designers should be aware that passing off someone else's design as your own breaks copyright law. Updating a design element that has been widely used for a long time – a polka dot, for instance – is unlikely to cause problems. Copying and pasting an existing design motif into your own work is another story and if you are reworking something that already exists, you should always aim to do so from scratch.

New developments in print and pattern tend to happen in small pockets, but they may get a high profile that leads to a significant influence over a far wider area. Of course, the spread of innovation in print is largely dependent on the customer's willingness to buy product with it on, or possibly industry's perception of this. Viewed from an external perspective, printed textile design seems to evolve quite gradually, shifting towards new styles by client or employer approval and customer consensus. It has been suggested that textile designers do not actually create completely original pattern or prints, but update styles that are already in existence. Whilst it is true that any image whatsoever can be somehow linked to something that has gone before, the idea does contain a kernel of truth. It is common for a brief to reference existing styles of pattern, for example, and it could be argued that commercial printed textiles do lean more heavily on their past than other design disciplines. Heritage and innovation are not mutually exclusive, however, and the ability to balance the two is a highly desirable skill.

Innovation from technology

Looking back at printed textile design over the last few hundred years reveals that one of the major factors affecting changes in the style of pattern is technological development. New printing methods, for example, tend to have a marked effect on the way practitioners work. This is fairly obvious – if the technology involved means that something new is possible with print and pattern, designers will want to try it out. Mindful of sales figures, it may be that they exploit some of the stylistic advances possible, but choose to work with existing content. The prevailing styles in print and pattern tend to change quite significantly as the major method of production does. This doesn't happen overnight; it can take some while for industry to feel confident enough with the new technology to really exploit it. Seen with benefit of hindsight and treated as a whole, printed textiles evolve fairly gently; this is not a field of design given to overnight revolutions. There are, however, designers who have had a significant impact on print by taking a more reactionary stance. As seen in Chapter one, William Morris's classic designs actively turned against prevailing technological and industrial advances.

From a digital perspective, it is important to recognize the influence that software has on the design process. Anyone who has spent any time designing with both Adobe® Photoshop® and Illustrator®, for example, will know that whist it is possible to do many of the same things in both programs, in practice the working process will be very different in both. This is chiefly because of the way they deal with images at their cores – Photoshop® works with pixels and Illustrator® with paths. However open and flexible any software is, it still has a fixed set of routes through which the process of manipulating an image is carried out. Of course, many new possibilities are opened up by working digitally, but it is important for designers to recognize that, however subconsciously it happens, it will have an effect on the way they work.

For new designers, one of the most exciting things about contemporary printed textiles is the gradual emergence of digital fabric printing. Whilst it could be argued that the technology is being over-hyped in the short term in some quarters (possibly this book among them), in the long term it does have the potential to profoundly change the way pattern can be printed onto cloth. It will take some time before the process is used commercially to anything like its full potential, but the designers of the future will play a big part in this.

Innovation from visual culture

Innovation in the way designs look can also come from other visual culture. During the 1950s, fine artists such as Jean Miró and Paul Klee were very influential on textile design. Scandinavian design also provided inspiration for many practitioners; possibly fuelled by post-war optimism and the rosy future that science suggested it could offer, some printed textile designers also looked to image sources such as crystallography or atomic structure. From these starting points of thin linear elements and simple abstract shapes, a style gradually evolved, often using textured effects that the advances in screen printing made more possible. In the 1960s, designers began to capitalize more on the flat colour effects facilitated by screen printing. Op Art was influential and some designers (such as Barbara Brown) looked at mathematical ways of constructing printed textile designs. The large-scale graphics of companies such as Marimekko (some of which remain in production to this day) helped to define a new style of print and pattern. The angled designs and colour palette that came to define the 1980s style (one that has been increasingly re-visited since the start of the twenty-first century by a whole range of creative practitioners) were in part derived from furniture design (in particular the Memphis company) and post-modern architecture (such as the work of Michael Graves and James Stirling).

Creating designs that innovate

Whilst it is important to point out that not everyone in the 1960s furnished their homes with large-scale abstract designs or wore designs by Bodymap in the 1980s, they are nonetheless periods when new design styles emerged. Some would argue that innovations in design tend to occur at times of economic buoyancy – companies feel confident about the future and are happy to offer their customers new, original patterns. In more austere times, manufacturers are less likely to take risks, reworking designs that have previously sold well that are felt to be reassuringly classic. Others postulate that innovation is more likely to occur in times of hardship – companies that take risks do better than ones that rest on their laurels. In practice, both are probably right to some degree and it is certainly possible to find examples of forward- and past-facing design from most points in time.

From the point of view of someone about to embark on a career in print and pattern, if you want your designs to innovate, it is important to develop an understanding of the way in which the boundaries of technology can be moved outwards. While a knowledge of the history of pattern is essential, for the innovator, so too is a constantly updated awareness of contemporary visual culture and a willingness to experiment with technology.

Juxtaposing print and product styles

In many cases, it is difficult for a printed textile designer to have much say in what product their designs will grace. Some print designers do start to develop their own product range, though, or collaborate with others, sharing the manufacturing and marketing costs, for example. In some instances, this process has been made less of a financial gamble with the development of digital manufacturing technology that allows products to be printed on demand rather than made and stored with no guarantee of sales.

Above:
The designs on these cushions by Thomas Paul combine historically influenced imagery with contemporary colour and composition.

It is worth having a look at how practitioners have created work that innovates by the juxtaposition of pattern and product. Even if you can't alter what the final product is, if you know what it is (and if the brief allows) you may be able to design a print or pattern that twists the visual language of the end-use. Just as you can twist existing styles by mixing apparently disparate elements together, so you can do the same by putting pattern associated with a particular product on something it isn't normally associated with it at all. An example of this might be a very traditional design on a garment with a very contemporary silhouette, or imagery that is not normally seen as being pattern on a product for the domestic interior.

Customer as designer

It is important to realize that products with print do not remain in isolation. Just as the final look of a pattern can be altered by its end-use, so can the customer twist it further by what they wear it with, or what other design is in the room with it. Very few people are dressed by stylists or have interior designers to do their furnishings. The looks customers develop themselves can be hugely influential - street style has had a massive effect on design since the 1950s.

The language of print

Every culture that uses imagery has its own visual language, and printed textile design is no exception. It has a history that dates back thousands of years and overlaps with many other areas of ornament and decoration. Attempting to catalogue all the styles that have ever existed in print, or to draw up an exhaustive list of all possible content that could be used in pattern would take an army of people years, so long and complex is its past. Some content (such as florals) remain in constant use, recurring season after season, appearing in a wide range styles that look to both the past and contemporary culture. Others only appear once in a while, returning for a different market for example when they can be re-contextualized in a way that makes them seem fresh or original.

Right:
Abbey Watkins's design blurs the boundaries between pattern and fashion illustration.

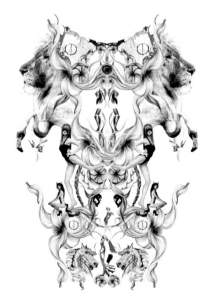

Chapter summary

The evolution of printed textiles is complex. It would be wrong to suggest that such a widespread design field has an overall direction that can be easily identified at any moment. However, there are identifiable trends within different markets and they often spill from one niche to another. Practitioners need to be able to work with a range of styles, but may also have to justify their use. Understanding the context they exist in is a vital part of this.

Pattern also evolves as a consequence of technical advances. Clearly digital technology is having an impact – styles have appeared in recent years that are a direct consequence of vector-based software, for example, and the possibilities of digital fabric printing are embryonic. In the long term, it is likely that much of the technology will change, but the idea at the heart of the industry remains the same: putting pattern on something can add to its desirability. To the designer, colour, style and content remain of paramount importance and their facility with them remains the reason for their employment.

Questions in summary

1. Which categories of visual content can print and pattern be divided into?

2. How can the designer create alternative colourways and a series of designs?

3. How can a printed textile designer produce original and innovative designs?

4. Why is it important for a print and pattern practitioner to be able to reference historical or retro design styles?

5. How can a practitioner balance commercial viability with originality and innovation?

6. How might the role of the printed textile designer evolve as a consequence of technological advances?

Working professionally

Every year, thousands of people from all over the world graduate from printed textile or surface pattern degrees and start to look for work. It is a highly competitive environment, and getting a break can seem a daunting prospect. This chapter aims to give some practical advice about how to maximize your chances. If you are serious about wanting a career in print or pattern, thinking about how you present your work beyond college or university is of paramount importance. This should start while you are still a student – testing your work on the outside world isn't something that needs to wait.

A good portfolio is vital. It doesn't only show you can design; it shows you understand the way the industry works and can deliver above and beyond what it wants.

Once you are in, there are an extraordinary number of directions your career could take you. Most printed textile designers are either employed, freelance or combine the two. Trying to work out which is best for you can be difficult, so the final part of this chapter looks at what each involves, and the factors you might want to think about when deciding which way to go.

The collection

Right:
These four designs, and the others on this page, form a collection of designs.

Designers normally work on collections rather than individual designs, creating groups of print and pattern linked by colour, style, content, presentation and end-use. Whilst the skill of creating an individual design is not to be underestimated, a potential employer or client will expect to see that you can design in collections. Aside from small craft-based or designer maker production, all parts of the industry produce a wide range of products, normally introduced for sale as collections themselves at key points in the year. The whole process revolves around a range of themes that are used to design and market whatever the products are. The idea of collections is at the core of it all, and print designers form an important part in driving it.

This section looks at what a collection is, and then gives practical advice on how to put one together. Practitioners can find themselves working on paper, fabric or digitally. Each has different requirements, but there are overarching factors in print and pattern collections that have to be considered if the individual designs are to successfully function as a collection.

What is a collection?

A collection is a group of designs that are based around the same theme or concept, normally in response to a brief. The number of designs in a collection varies a lot, but is typically eight or more. (In theory, however, it could be two or more designs.) The print designs can either be for a single company to use across a range of their products (a Spring Summer swimwear collection, for example, or a range of stationery products), or created to sell individually (via an agency, for example). In most cases, a professional brief will result in a collection rather than an individual design.

'The details are not the details. They make the design.'

Charles Eames

Colour

A collection of designs should use the same colour palette, although not every design need use every colour of the palette. In most cases, the colour tends to be used in a similar way. If there is a bright colour that is used as an accent colour in one design, it is likely to be used in the same way in any other design (rather than as a large expanse of colour). More than any other factor, colour will tie your collection together.

Content

All the designs in a collection should have similar content. This tends to come quite naturally from the theme or inspiration behind them. If you are designing a collection of designs that are all to be used by the same company, it is normally okay to use the same element in more than one design (provided they are happy with your doing this). However, if you are designing freelance and the collection is for general sale (rather than to commission), every element in the design must be unique. If you have used a drawing of a leaf, for example, you could not use the same drawing in another design (but it would be fine to use a different drawing).

Style

The collection should have an overarching style. As with the content, this will probably follow naturally from the inspiration or the brief (in fact the style and content may be fairly inseparable from each other). Take care not to have one or more designs that do something very different from the rest.

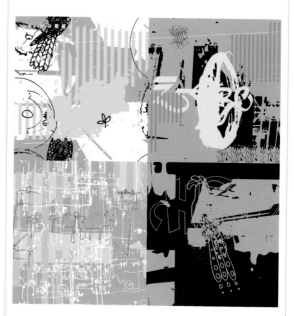

Presentation

There are a number of different ways to present a collection. The methods will normally be governed by the brief; also highly significant is whether the individual designs are on paper, fabric or digital media and what the end-use will be. Whatever the methods, it is crucial that it is consistent across the whole collection, and that it shows it to its best advantage.

Left:
The designs in this collection of designs share the same colour palette. The content is unique in each design, but derived from the same inspiration sources.

Getting started on a collection

In many ways, working on a collection can be easier than working on a single design. Many designers work backwards and forwards across the collection, moving from one design to another if they get stuck, for example. The process described in the following section is essentially one of getting as much as possible needed to build the collection ready to work with, before starting the final designs. This can be a very efficient way of working and can really help with time management.

Colour

For many designers, getting the colour palette established is the first step in designing a collection. If you are working in paint, mixing up a supply of each colour can significantly improve workflow; when working digitally, setting up and saving the palette has the same benefit (via Swatches in Photoshop® or Illustrator®, for example). The palette may be part of the brief, but if it isn't, devising your own colour palette should be a crucial early stage in building a collection. The advent of digital printing potentially eliminates the need for finite palettes of fixed colours, but the brief is still likely to require some form of colour mood or atmosphere. If part of the brief involves doing colourways, you should also get the palette that they will need ready to go. Remember the vital part colour has in getting the style or atmosphere of a design right, and the crucial role the proportion of colour plays in this.

Right:
This range of elements was developed alongside a wide variety of others to form an entire collection.

Opposite:
The final design, created from the various elements.

Inspiration

Sourcing the inspiration for a collection is essentially a research process. It is important to make sure that you have enough material to support the whole collection, particularly if it involves a lot of designs. You should remember to keep at least some of the key source images in easy view at all times and regularly re-read the brief to prevent you going off on a tangent. For many professional designers, the development stage doesn't really exist as a discrete entity – they go straight from the inspiration to final designs. This takes some practice and is largely down to the tight deadlines normally involved. (Some designers who work this way create more final designs than the brief requires, pruning the collection down at the end to ensure its quality.)

Elements / content

Although you can work on each design sequentially from start to finish, many designers prefer to work on the collection as a whole. One of the key ways you can do this is to get as much of the content ready to go before you start. If you are working digitally, for example, using scans of your own hand-drawn images, you could do all the drawings first, scan them all in, and then start putting the different elements together in the designs, experimenting with which ones work best together. It is important to get the balance right when working this way – there should be room for reflection and experiment; you must be able to make quality judgements as you progress, and not be afraid to bring in new content if you don't have enough. It is very important to make sure the style of the final designs is right – the elements you develop must reflect the style that the brief requires.

AUTHOR TIP
GETTING UNSTUCK

No matter how experienced they are, all designers experience moments when nothing seems to go right. Maybe inspiration seems impossible to find, or every visual experiment appears to be no good. However terrible this seems at the time, good designers learn to work through it. You just have to keep making work without worrying about how good it is (which is harder than it sounds).

The best way of doing this is often just to do a lot. For example, set yourself a target of doing 50 drawings in an hour. Many of the drawings may be no good, but in almost all cases, some of them will suggest a way forward. If they don't, try doing something completely different (working with another medium, for example) and then come back to the first set later. Everyone gets stuck, and being able to dig yourself out of the hole is a key design skill.

Product and illustrations

If you know what product the design is going to be used on, it should be part of the design process from the start. It is a good idea to get hold of images of what the product range is, or draw it if that isn't possible, and place the designs on the product images to create illustrations as you go. If you aren't sure of the end-use, it can be a good idea to pick one or more suitable products to visualize it on. In this case it is fine to use the same product for a whole collection. In other words, you might show all the designs on the same garment flat.

5

1

5

3

   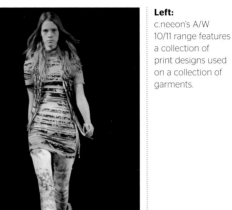

Left:
c.neeon's A/W 10/11 range features a collection of print designs used on a collection of garments.

'Of course, there will always be those who look only at technique, who ask "how", while others of a more curious nature will ask "why". Personally, I have always preferred inspiration to information.'

Man Ray

  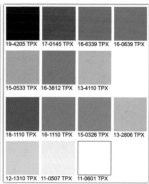 

Reference: arthd001a   Repeat: 64cm x 64cm block
                            No. of colours: 7 (6 plus 1 base colour)

Referencing designs

If you are working for a company, they will probably have some kind of referencing system for your designs. If you are working freelance, you must devise your own system and it is a good idea to get into the habit of this while you are a student. Referencing makes it much easier to describe the design or designs in any correspondence and helps you to catalogue your work – you can save the design using its reference number as a file name, for example. How you do this is up to you. All that matters is that each design has its own unique number. A collection of designs would normally be sequentially numbered.

Creating a collection of designs

By this stage, you will have almost certainly decided whether the collection is going to be on paper or on fabric. This is likely to be determined by your working environment or by the brief. If you are working from home on a self-generated brief to fill a perceived gap in your folio prior to an interview and are worried that you have no access to screen-printing equipment, don't panic. A lot of practitioners never actually work directly onto fabric. Equally, some designers will almost always work onto fabric – some design studios create all their designs as blanks or samples.

Unless you are told otherwise, the final designs that make up a collection must be actual size. In other words, if it would be 50cm high in use on a garment, it should be 50cm high on paper or fabric. If the designs are going to be in repeat, you should show at least 5cm (approximately 2in) of this on one side and on the bottom (if you're designing in 2x2 repeat anyway – this won't be a problem). An exception to working full scale right from the start may be when using vector-based software (such as Illustrator®) that allows designs to be infinitely rescaled; in all other circumstances, assume you should design to the size the prints will be in use. If you are using pixel-based software (such as Photoshop®), design at 300dpi unless told differently.

How you present the final collection and what it comprises will vary depending on the brief and whether it is paper or fabric based. Details on actual presentation are given on page 149; what follows are suggestions of what you should consider for paper- and fabric-based collections in terms of actually creating the final designs. If you are asked to create a collection in digital format (if the client wants files rather than print-outs or fabric samples), the collection will probably follow a similar route to the paper-based one, but a few extra pointers are given below.

Above:
The back of the furnishing design shown on page 148 would show the design in repeat (with details), a colourway, the palette as colour chips, an illustration of potential use and a reference number.

Paper-based collections

These can be either hand drawn or painted, or done digitally. Whilst collections might feature a mix of techniques, this should be within the designs themselves. Having some designs in a collection that are entirely digital and some that are done completely by hand is not generally a good idea. (You can get round this by scanning in the hand-made stuff, tweaking the colours digitally to the same palette as the digital ones and then printing them out.)

The collection may need to include colourways, illustrations of how it will (or could) appear in end-use and (if it is in repeat) how an expanse of the design will look (normally two repeats in either direction). You may also be asked to provide co-ordinates, or chips (small squares) of each colour in the palette. It is recommended that you don't leave any of these extras until the end – if you are doing some of them, do so as you work on the main designs. You should also work out the format you will use to present them, and stick to it for the whole collection.

Fabric-based collections

These can be generated in a number of different ways. Sometimes the print process is only at the very end – the designer might create the collection on computer, say, and print a digital fabric sample of each design at the end of the process. In other cases, a more hands-on approach might be taken, with designers using pre-prepared pattern elements on screens to print with. Several designers may be involved in such a process. If the designs are screen printed, the dyestuff is likely to be mixed up in advance according to the colour palette and used for the whole collection.

Printed textile designs on fabric are normally shown as either samples or blanks. A sample is just a rectangular bit of fabric with the design printed on it. They are used for both home/interiors and fashion collections. A blank (sometimes known as a front) is a simple mock up of a garment (normally its front), generally featuring a couple of fabrics and a suggestion of detailing. These are only used for fashion collections.

As with paper-based collections, the designs should be to scale and may be accompanied by a digital file of the designs. Illustrations and colour chips of the palette are relatively uncommon, but colourways may be included (more often with samples than blanks). If the design is in repeat, the sample would normally be big enough to show this.

Digital collections

Digital collections are likely to have the same content as a paper-based collection. Designers working in this way should check they are working in the correct file format (there may be more than one) and that the designs are the correct (full) scale from the start. Very specific requirements may be given about how the designs should be supplied. This will depend on the brief, but might involve (say) Photoshop® files with each colour on a separate Layer, or the designs to be delivered showing two repeats in either direction.

Even if you don't have to show the collection on paper or fabric, you may still be asked to put together some kind of presentation package (a PowerPoint®, for example).

The portfolio

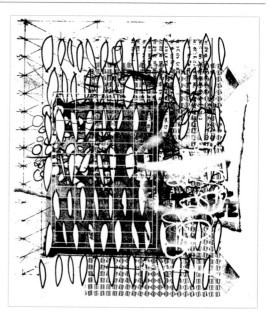

In order to get started on a career in printed textile design, you need a portfolio. Whether you are trying to get a design job with a company, or looking for representation with an agency, your folio is ultimately what will get you the job.

There are two factors at play here. Clearly the content is vital - you need to show that you can create individual designs, but presentation is also crucial; not only will it set your work off to its best advantage, but it can speak volumes about your understanding about the needs of your potential client or employer.

Importantly - and this is probably one of the most common features missing from student portfolios - your portfolio should show you can design in different ways.

What is a portfolio?

The portfolio is a well-presented selection of your work. It is normally used when applying for a job, or selling designs or design services. If it is put together for an interview, it needs to act as a showcase of your design skills. If you are using it to sell your work, or to pitch for a commission, it should reflect the needs of the client.

As it is the single most important factor in getting or selling work, it must be completely professional and should show your work off to its best advantage. Think about the viewer - they should quickly be able to see where your talents lie, without being distracted by poor or over-fussy presentation. It is worth investing in a decent folio - good quality ones last for years.

Tips for creating a portfolio

Keep it simple and consistent. Use pure white as a background, either to print out on or mount onto. Don't be afraid of empty space - try not to pack too much onto each sheet. If the work is not presented in plastic sheets (and hence all the same size), try to use as few sizes as possible. Make sure the work is the right way up and keep everything (or as much as possible) either portrait or landscape - it looks bad if you have to keep turning the folio round. A3 (tabloid) or a little bit bigger is the most common size for fashion-focused textile designs; interior and furnishing designs tend to be larger and are hence often shown in an A1 (D) folio. If you're using text, limit the number of fonts and font sizes and make sure they reflect the work. It's better to have less work of a higher standard than to try and pack in everything you've ever done (don't give people the chance to remember you for the bad stuff).

Make sure it's editable. The format you use should allow you to add or remove work without difficulty. This might mean avoiding page numbering or double sided printing, but the exception to this might be a small package of designs you put together to showcase your work; as you are likely to send this out rather than show it in person, you can just keep the master version as a digital file and update it when you need to. If work is hand mounted, make sure you can change the mount if it gets worn or damaged. Part of the function of a mount is to protect the artwork.

Decide on a format for the portfolio and stick to it. So long as it looks good, it doesn't matter if you put it together digitally or by hand. Provided it doesn't look too jumbled, it is fine to mix both. When working digitally, use software you know how to use (don't try and learn something new the night before an interview), set up a basic template and sample print-out quality (ideally use inkjet printers on coated paper). If you do it by hand, use the right tools (guillotines or very sharp scalpels) to make sure everything is correctly aligned (lay everything out and check it looks okay before you start sticking it down).

Keep other people's work to a minimum (only a few examples on inspiration pages, for example). For copyright reasons, you must credit it - using a very small (but legible) font size and putting the text vertically up one edge of the image in question is fine. Never, ever try to pass off other people's work as your own.

You need to take your time to put everything together. Don't leave it to the last minute or underestimate how long this can take. Your portfolio should be regularly updated - there's nothing wrong with doing some new designs especially for it. These should be in collections, however - don't have individual designs floating about. It should also be ready for show at a moment's notice - get it ready when you have plenty of time. Good work can be ruined by poor presentation.

Right:
This furnishing design features a 64cm x 64cm (25.1in x 25.1in) repeat. It is printed out with 6cm (2.3in) of the repeat on the side and bottom.

Presenting paperwork

It is quite usual for print designers to present their work on paper, either in the form of the original artwork (if the design was done by hand) or as high-quality prints (if the work is digital). Broadly speaking, there are two ways you can do this. If you are showing your work in order to sell it (at a trade fair, for example) or purely to show your ability to design print and pattern (at an interview with an agency or a potential employer, for instance), you probably don't need to show any development work at all (unless told otherwise). You just show final designs, presented to scale. If you are asked to show development work, or if you are going for a job that requires you to apply your skills a little more widely than pure printed textile design, you should take a more narrative approach to visually explaining how the final designs came about.

This type of presentation is normally shown in plastic sheets. You'd slide each sheet from one side of the opened portfolio to the other, allowing your audience to pull out any work they were particularly interested in.

Presenting final designs

Standpoints on mounting vary, but unless told otherwise, the following points should see you through. If the design is smaller than A1 (D), it should have a border of some sort, either by mounting it onto a larger piece of paper or card, or by printing it out with white space around the edges. Across the whole folio, it is better not to have more than three different sizes of mounted work or printouts; ideally aim for one or two. Work that is very large can be folded down, ideally so part of the design remains visible and can be shown unmounted or without a border.

If the design is digital, it is normally fine to print it onto coated heavy paper or card (anything over about 165gsm should be fine), leaving a border round the edge. Provided you do it really neatly, it is okay to join printouts together if you have a big design and you don't have access to a large-format printer. Note that this can be a time-consuming and fiddly process; it may be quicker (if more expensive) to find a printer who will do it for you. Unless asked otherwise, always print onto matte coated paper with an inkjet printer. If you're printing out a lot, don't underestimate how long this will take and how much this could cost. If the design is on a white or very pale ground, it can be useful to put a very thin black line around it to make it clear where the design stops and the border starts. (Keep this exactly the same size whenever you use it.)

Mounting materials

If you have done work by hand (or have been specifically asked to mount digital work), you should mount on pure, smooth white cartridge paper or thin card. Don't use mountboard or foamboard - it will cost a fortune and your folio will either weigh a tonne or be as thick as it is wide. The exception to this is if you have been asked to prepare boards to do a visual presentation to a group of people and you need to stand them upright. Cut the artwork down to the size you need it using a metal ruler and a scalpel or a guillotine. If using the former method, always place the ruler so it covers what you want to keep - if you accidentally move away from it with the knife, you'll cut into the waste parts, not the important bit. If the artwork doesn't need cutting down but looks a bit shabby, it can still be worth taking a whisker off each edge - this will often smarten it up. Use a square of wide, good quality double-sided tape in each corner of the back of the design to stick it to the mount. If you want to make the design re-mountable, stick a square of paper or sticky-backed plastic to the corners of the design first - that way you can pull the mount off without damaging the design itself.

Additional items to present

Printed textile designers working for furnishing or home / interiors should put nothing other than the design on the front. Furnishing designs sometimes show the colour palette as chips of each featured colour on the back. Also on the back, they could feature a colourway or two (all or part of the design scaled down), a visualization (illustration of end-use) and a 2x2 repeat. These should all be the same size - about 10cm (approximately 4in) square is fine. If you are printing out a digital design, it is fine to stick all of these on the back. Be consistent about how you do this, particularly with regard to size and placement.

Right and opposite:
These designs by Joasia Staszek place elements of presentation layout and art direction into a textiles context.

If you are working for fashion, then the colourway(s), visualization(s) and 2x2 repeats (if appropriate) can be mounted or laid out below the design (that is, on the front rather than the back). Unless asked, you don't need colour chips of the palette. The visualization doesn't have to be a detailed illustration - a fairly simple flat or two can really help to contextualize the design and is highly recommended. These can be a bit smaller than for home / interiors, but don't make them much less than 8cm (approximately 3in) square. Use a very thin black line around the edge if there is any white in the design or the ground. As before, be consistent about the size and location of them across the portfolio. If you are designing for another sector such as giftware, go with the fashion way of putting the extras on the front unless you are told otherwise.

Presentation of a whole project

In some cases, you may be asked to present your work in a way that explains where the ideas came from. There can be a number of reasons for this, the most common of which is to reassure your client or employer of the validity of the collection and its success in answering the brief. Note that in many professional instances, the process of how you get to the final design is probably only of interest to you. Presentation and discussion should focus on the ability of your print and pattern to do the job asked of it. If conversation turns to how the ideas were developed, it is fine to give a few details, but the main focus should still be the final designs. An example of when this might happen may be part of getting a job. It is quite usual for companies to give prospective new recruits a test brief as part of the recruitment process. This will often involve presenting some inspiration and development work in addition to any final designs.

The content will vary with the brief, but typically this type of presentation might require any or all of the following: inspiration, colour palette, fabrics / textile designs, product direction and then the final collection, possibly illustrated in projected end-use. Final designs might not need to be shown full scale, but you should still create them that way, then scale down a copy for the presentation. You may also cover market research / client profile, technical information and finishing. In general, the layout should be styled, subtly reflecting the theme of the collection.

Layouts can be done by hand or digitally or a mix of both. Fabric samples can be included, but are normally quite small; they can cover sourced fabric as well as fabric you've created.

It is normal for this type of presentation to be shown in plastic sheets in a ring-bound folio. A landscape format is more common than portrait; the whole folio should use one or the other.

Text can be used. Be consistent with the fonts and their sizes and make sure the style of the font fits the theme of the work. It must also be easy to read – it's fairly common to have the title in a more artistic or styled font and the main text in something simple like Helvetica or Arial. If you use hand-written text, it must be legible. Don't number the pages unless you're presenting the work as a finished trend or look book – you might need to change the running order or add or remove stuff.

Presenting digitally

It is increasingly commonplace for designers to show their work digitally. This could be a relatively simple slide show featuring photos or re-sized digital files, or it might involve sophisticated layout using software such as InDesign®. You must ensure that the intended viewer can actually open the file(s) and quickly and easily view your work - if they have to instal new software or sit through a pointless introductory animation, they are unlikely to bother to actually look at your designs, particularly if they have 30 other applications to look at.

There are essentially three ways of showing your work digitally. Firstly, you might do a presentation in person, using PowerPoint® for example. Secondly, you might put together a package of some sort to send - a CD of images, for example, or a PDF with highlights of your folio. Finally, there is the online presence - a website featuring a collection of your work. This can be a full site, but many designers use blogs and this is recommended if you are looking for an initial way to get your work on the web.

Any designs you show in a package or online should never be full size - scaling down the whole design or a good part of it to about 500 pixels square is normally fine. They should have your name, the copyright symbol, the word copyright and the year they were created (Your Name © Copyright 2011) subtly placed onto them (you can do this with a semi-transparent Layer in Photoshop®, for example). This will ensure that people can clearly see your work on screen, but that the designs will be too small to use without your knowledge.

Presenting fabric samples and blanks

If you create final designs on fabric, there are generally two ways you can present them. The first of these is fairly straightforward - as a sample fabric. However, if you are working in fashion, some textile design studios use another method. When they are showing designs to potential clients, they use blanks. These are quite simple fabric shapes, normally designed to look like the front of a potential garment.

In either case, the fabric should show the design at the scale it is intended to be used. Designs are normally stored or transported carefully rolled up in collections and then placed in a box or small suitcase, although studios carrying many hundreds of designs may have everything on hangers of some sort and use rails. You should have scans or good quality photographs of your fabric samples to hand, so you can show the work online, for example.

‘**Technology is making design more exciting, with colour, wallpaper, textures, fabrics that could never have been created without the technology.**’

David Bromstad

Samples

Fabric samples are normally shown mounted on headers. This is a strip of card, folded along its length. The top of the fabric is then inserted into the fold and attached to it. It is fairly usual for headers to have hangers, so large numbers of samples can be hung on a rail for presentation or storage purposes. You should aim to have all your headers the same height (about 8 to 10 cm (3-4in) is typical) and as few different widths as possible (ideally just one). The pure white card they are made from should be the same across the whole folio and needs to be sturdy enough to support the weight of the fabric it holds. Although some studios use branded headers, stick to plain white to start with. Very large fabric samples are sometime folded in half vertically and then placed in the header. Samples are normally no smaller that A4 (letter) size, but can be a lot bigger, particularly with furnishing fabrics that have a large repeat.

The fabric itself should be pressed and trimmed carefully so each edge is as straight as possible. Edges are normally prevented from fraying by ironing interfacing onto the back and then cutting down the middle of it; some designers use good quality clear adhesive tape to do this. In some instances edges are overlocked or even hemmed. A number of different methods are used to attach the cloth to the header; very strong double-sided tape is probably the easiest.

The reference number for the design will either be on a sticker on the back of the fabric (generally only if the fabric is opaque) or on the back of the header. This may sometimes also contain some technical information about the print – what techniques were used, for example, or the dyestuff involved.

Blanks

Blanks are intended to suggest some sort of context that the printed textile design could be used in. This is normally done by making the fabric (or a combination of fabrics) into what resembles the front of a garment (blanks are sometimes referred to as fronts). There is no set format for a blank, but they often include at least two different textiles (one of which could be plain) and some suggestion of detailing or trim (a few buttons, say). The styling of the blank will reflect the look of the print (or occasionally, it will intentionally give it a twist). The construction tends to be fairly basic, but should not detract from the quality of the printed fabric. If you want to show your designs in this way, you will need to invest some time at the machines to ensure your sewing skills are good enough.

Blanks may be mounted on headers or some sort of hanger; this will depend on how they are made, but should be consistent across the whole folio. The reference number (and possibly printing details) may be included on a small label on the back or on the header if there is one.

The world of work

Above:
A design from the freelance portfolio of Lucy O'Brien.

When you are thinking about becoming a professional printed textile designer, it can be useful to take a good look at your own practice and working methods to help decide which part or parts of the industry you want to work for. Getting started is difficult and it is very important that you can show a potential employer or client that you have something to offer. Ideally, you should also be looking to work in a way that you know will prove stimulating and interesting, although in the early days of a career any experience is good experience.

Whilst you might have a very focused idea of who your folio is for (print for menswear, for example), it can be good to try to work out as many different end-uses for your work as possible.

Freelancing or employment?

When setting out on a career in printed textile design, one of the most important decisions to make is whether to be employed or to work freelance. In practice, many designers switch between the two at various points in their career, and it is not uncommon for some to do a bit of both. Deciding which way to go should reflect the way you work as well as who you want to design for.

Employment

Employment normally involves working for a company or a studio. You are paid a salary (normally monthly) and your employer makes tax contributions on your behalf. You may be entitled to some kind of pension or other benefits beyond the ones provided by the state. Working for an employer can involve working set hours (although they might be quite long), and you are entitled to government-set minimum amounts of pay, holiday, sickness leave, maternity / paternity leave and so on.

At a junior or trainee level, the work tends to be very structured, and for many people starting out, this is part of the appeal – you gain experience of the industry as you earn a regular wage. Once you feel ready or willing to take on additional responsibilities, there may be the opportunity within the same organization for promotion; if not, you may feel the time is right to look for a new employer who can offer you a post to further your career.

For many people, the security of a regular income and the possibility of a fairly well defined career path are the most important factors in seeking employment. Although any work in the textiles industry involves a degree of collaboration, team working skills are crucial in employment (and likely to come up at interview).

Freelancing

Freelance designers either work through an agency or studio, or directly with clients. In most cases, the amount they earn is dependent on the designs they sell or are commissioned to do. (The exceptions to this are studios that pay a retainer to their freelancers.) You are responsible for your own book-keeping, invoicing your agent or clients and all the other business administration. The hours you work are ultimately up to you; most freelancers work very long hours, particularly when they start out.

Although some freelancers start working directly with clients, it is more normal to start with an agency. Projects for clients or agency commissions will be to set briefs; some agencies may offer more scope for individual interpretation in the work you do for the folio they carry for speculative sales. It is likely you will work for a broader range of markets or end-uses than if you are employed. Established freelancers may be able to be more selective about the work they do; many agents or studio managers are ex-freelancers.

Freelancing requires a high level of self-motivation, particularly if you work in your own studio or at home. For some people, this can prove lonely. It is likely to take some time to earn a decent income; you may need another job to pay the bills while you are starting out. Possibly for this reason, many freelancers start out in employment, although some work this way straight from graduation.

Above:
Freelance designers may collaborate with companies such as Graniph.

The CV or résumé

Your Curriculum Vitae (or résumé) is vital to your career and it is worth spending some time getting it right. It should be regularly updated to reflect your experience and skills. It is also worthwhile having a number of different versions, particularly if you are at the start of your career and looking at a wide range of possible opportunities. For instance, you might have three different CVs – one with a fashion print angle, one for furnishing and another for trend prediction. In some cases, you will be asked to complete an application form rather than submit a CV, but this is likely to involve a lot of the same information.

It must have no spelling or grammatical mistakes – this is inexcusable and may result in your CV going straight in the bin. Don't rely on a software spell check; read it through word by word and ideally ask someone else to double-check it. Unless you are told otherwise, a CV should fit on two sides of A4 (letter). The layout must be clear and unfussy. Think about the person who will be reading it – can they quickly and easily get the information they need from it? It should be word processed, although you may sometimes be asked for it in PDF format. If you print it out (rather than submitting it online), make sure it is a good-quality print on decent paper.

'Find a job you like and you add five days to every week.'

H. Jackson Brown, Jr.

The layout is really important – you are promoting yourself as a designer and this should be reflected in a well-designed, easily navigable document. Be consistent – use the same font in the same size, and do all your titles (Contacts, Education etc.) in the same way. It is a good idea to stick to this format for the covering letter and an image package too. Use an easy-to-read font and keep the text black (on a white ground). A CV or résumé should contain the following information:

Contact / Personal details

Your name, your address (if you are living in student accommodation, it can be better to put a more permanent contact down such as a parental address), your phone number(s), an e-mail address (that you check regularly and that sounds professional) and webspace(s) if you have your portfolio online (you should). This section normally includes your date of birth and nationally as well.

Skills summary / Personal profile

A few bullet points (four or five) or a short statement (about 50 words in either case) that outlines your key attributes, ideally with evidence. Try to use as many positive keywords as you can and make sure that the evidence is drawn from a variety of sources (not all from university or the same job). These must be relevant to the position or company.

Career objectives

A short statement about what sort of job you want. Be specific, and (obviously) tailor it to the job you are applying for. This might be part of the previous section.

Education

This is normally presented in reverse order (so the most recent at the top). It is generally divided into three columns: dates attended, name of institution / place, qualification (including grades) with brief details such as subjects covered. You only need to go back as far as secondary school (high school).

Employment / work experience / voluntary work

This is sometimes divided into different sections, but when you are starting out, it is fine to group it together. As with education, it should be in reverse date order (most recent at top), and have three columns: dates, employer / brief address and responsibilities / duties, including job title. These don't necessarily have to be directly linked to textiles - if you have worked in a different field and the job demonstrates a skill you think prospective employers might be interested in, include it. If you are a freelancer, give a client list (this is probably the most important part of a freelance CV - some designers have it in a separate section).

Additional skills / information

A list of skills or relevant information you haven't included elsewhere on the CV. These can be grouped into sections such as IT / CAD / software skills, textile skills, general art / design skills, language skills, driving licence. If you've won or been shortlisted for any awards or competitions, describe that here too.

Interests

A brief list of what you do in your spare time, with interesting details and any responsibilities involved.

References

Normally two people, one of whom should be your last or current employer. If you are a student or relatively recent graduate, the other should be from your current or last educational institution. Give their name, job title and full, correct contact details. Always make sure you ask the people concerned. It is normally fine to put 'Available on request' instead of naming people, particularly if it is a speculative application, but you should always provide referees if asked.

Getting a job

Getting a job, particularly your first one in the industry, can be very difficult. You need to be patient and very proactive in promoting yourself - some employers do much of their recruitment through speculative job applications rather than, say, advertising posts openly. Work experience, a strong CV and a portfolio that shows you could do the job are vital.

Portfolio

This is at the heart of getting a job. Having a good one is only half the battle - you also need to get it seen. Get an online presence via a website or a blog or an image-hosting site like Flickr. Make sure it is easy to see your work and that it is professional in content and tone. Put together a design package of a few beautifully laid-out sheets of your work (a maximum of four designs per page is normally about right) clearly labelled and with a copyright statement. You can send these out with a CV and a covering letter to potential employers or employment agencies. In some cases, the first step of the application process will require this anyway. Another method of doing this is via a CD containing sample images or a presentation.

Right:
Catalogues from trade fairs such as Première Vision are useful for getting lists of agents.

Contacts

There's an old cliché that says it's not what you know, but who you know. This is a fairly fundamental truth in the design business. Networking and making contacts is crucial; your contacts list is probably as useful as your portfolio. Exchange business cards with everyone you meet professionally and catalogue all the ones you receive. Write down names you are given over the phone or recommended in conversation and make sure you have a (backed-up) e-mail address book. An increasing number of practitioners use social networking websites – Linked In (www.linkedin.com) is probably the most widely used professional one, although some designers do use Facebook (www.facebook.com) (if you do, keep any personal use on a completely separate account). You should keep in contact too via occasional updates or invitations to see new examples of your designs online.

Job research

Actually finding where jobs are advertised can require a bit of work. Traditionally this is often done via the trade press (*Drapers Record* in the UK, or fibre2fashion in the US, for example, carry a wide range of fashion industry jobs). Many companies now have a section of their website devoted to recruitment. Make a list of every company you think you could work for and trawl through them all, checking back regularly for any updates. Recruitment agencies are used a lot by the industry and there are a number of specialist ones for (say) the retail or creative sectors.

The elevator pitch

This is an old business adage: if you found yourself in a lift with your dream employer and you had a couple of floors' worth of time before they got out, could you tell them what you do? A surprising number of graduates struggle to actually tell people what their practice is in 20 words or less. If you don't know what you do and what makes you unique, it is unlikely you will be able to tell anyone else.

Promote your work

Try to get your work seen as widely as possible. Look for competitions or opportunities to showcase your work online. Try to get your work featured in other people's blogs or even magazines or books. It's unlikely you'll get paid for this, but it might lead to work of some sort and at the very least will help to raise your profile. Find people to collaborate with, both in terms of creating new work and publicizing it.

Covering letter

When you contact someone to ask about employment opportunities, it is standard practice to do this via a covering letter or e-mail (the exception to this may be if the initial step for a post is via an application form). Broadly speaking, this should do three things: show that you know a bit about the company, explain why you are approaching them and why you think they should employ you. This should be very focused on the company you are sending it to.

Getting an agent

Possibly one of the most frequently asked questions by graduating designers (or existing practitioners thinking of going freelance) is how to get an agent. Getting representation is ultimately down to being able to show your work to an agency and them then deciding whether or not they can sell your work to their clients. Different agencies are looking for very different things and what one sees as being highly viable commercially may be complete anathema to another. Although agencies do advertise vacancies from time to time in the trade press, most receive enough speculative enquiries not to have to do this. Some agencies have a history of taking on people who have done placements with them first. If you have such experience (and it was a positive one), it is definitely worth trying to set up an opportunity to show your work. If you haven't worked with an agency before (and you can afford to do this), it is definitely worth asking for a placement or internship.

Finding agents

To start with, draw up a list of agencies that you think might be interested in your work. Try and get hold of catalogues for trade fairs where some of the exhibitors are either agents or freelance studios. It is important to bear in mind that some of these exhibitors will be designers who only show their own work and do not represent others. Likely trade fairs include Indigo (part of Première Vision), Heimtextil and Surtex.

In some cases, contact details of the exhibitors may also get posted on the web. Ideally, however, you should actually visit a fair - this will give you the chance to research potential representation relatively easily. You may not be able to speak to any of the agencies directly; they have paid a lot of money for their space and are there to sell, so don't be offended if they give you short shrift. However, you should be able to see the sort of design work they sell and gauge if it fits your own. It is probably a mistake to try to show them your work there and then. If their stand looks quiet, however, you can offer a CV (résumé) and try to make an appointment to visit them at a later date.

If you cannot visit a fair, you should try to find out a bit about the agency to ensure you are not wasting effort. For example, some only work with fashion clients, or only knitwear, or only kids' wear; if your portfolio is for furnishing, there is no point in contacting them. It is also important to understand that not all agents exhibit at fairs; some only work directly with clients. Websites aren't always particularly helpful, although some will go as far as providing instructions for prospective designers to send in work. When making a list, try to think internationally - it is increasingly normal for designers to have representation in a different country from their own.

Approaching agencies

Once you have a list of potential contacts, you should carefully prepare a selection of your work with which to make the initial approach. There are any number of methods of doing this, but unless the agency's website specifies otherwise, sending unsolicited e-mails full of large attachments is not recommended. In general, you should send three things. Firstly, a beautifully packaged selection of about eight or 10 designs, either printed onto A4 (letter) paper or on an easily accessible CD. Secondly, an accompanying letter that demonstrates you understand what the agency does and why you think your work fits their profile. Finally, an up-to-date, perfectly laid out CV (résumé). All three items should be presented in the same style.

Now you need patience. Don't expect replies, but they will contact you if they like your work. This stage can be very demoralizing, but try to hold onto the thought that if agencies think they can sell your work, they will want to. If you haven't heard anything after a few weeks, try to pluck up the courage to pick up the phone, call the agency, ask if they've had a chance to look at your work and see if you can make an appointment to show them your full portfolio. If this doesn't get you anywhere, make sure to ask if they know of anyone else who might be interested - a contact with a personal recommendation is a very good contact indeed.

In rare cases, you may get taken on immediately (this is more likely with overseas agencies), but it is more typical to be invited to an interview with a portfolio. When you are putting your folio together, remember that the agency will be looking for work they can sell to their clients - if you've been able to find out a bit about the agency, your work should reflect their audience. This should also come across in any interview or discussion, along with an awareness of current designers, markets and trends.

Money matters

Whether you are working for an employer or freelance, part of the recruitment, selling or pitching process will involve financial discussion or negotiation. A common graduate mistake is to be unprepared for this. Given that the result could have an effect on how much money you have in your pocket for some time to come, it is worth giving it a bit of forethought.

If the job is advertised, the salary will normally be given, possibly as a range dependent on experience. If you are shortlisted for a job, there may be some discussion of the salary at interview. Other companies do this at the point of making the job offer to you - this is the best possible moment to try and get an improved offer. If there is no mention of the wage prior to interview, it is professional to bring it up, but you should have a figure in mind if you do this. Your job search will probably give you a good idea of what to go for, but if not, look at the adverts for similar posts to get an idea.

If you are freelancing with an agency, they will probably have a set commission they take, which is not normally negotiable. Some agencies take a smaller commission, but charge for taking the work to a trade fair or a selection of clients - if your work sells, you do better, but you lose money if it doesn't. Most agencies have set pricing structures and charge roughly the same amount as each other (see the tip box on page 187 for a brief guide to pricing work). You should establish with the agency if they are okay with you working for your own clients, an employer or other agencies from the start - a contract may be involved that sets this down in writing.

When freelancing directly with a company - creating a collection to commission, for example - you must sort out a price before starting any work. If it is a big job, requires a lot of expenditure on your part or if you have not worked with the client before, you might ask for a part-payment up front, or staged payments as certain parts of the work are completed. Be aware, however, that some clients will just assume you'll invoice for the whole job when it is done and may be slightly put out if you suggest doing it another way. It is also vital to be absolutely clear about what the work will entail and how it will be signed off - it is quite common for a client to ask a designer to make a number of alterations after a job has been supposedly finished. It is much better to sort out beforehand that any further changes must be paid for once they have signed it off, rather than try and negotiate this as the requests for tweaks come in.

Left:
For a freelance design such as this one, an agency will typically take a commission of about 40-45 per cent on each design they sell.

Trade fairs

One of the best ways to find out about how the
industry works is to visit a trade fair. These can
seem very impenetrable the first time you visit
one; it is important to do a bit of research to find
out exactly what is going on.

A trade fair is a business-to-business event.
Some fairs are very strict on who is allowed to
attend (such as Bread and Butter), others are more
flexible and may even have special student days
(Première Vision, for example). Each one targets a
specific part of the production process, although
some of the large ones may actually be a range of
different fairs.

The ones of most interest to printed textile
designers are probably the ones where studios,
agencies or freelance designers show, such as
Indigo, a part of Première Vision which focuses
on textile design for fashion, or Heimtextil, which
concentrates on designs for home / interiors.
Agencies exhibit hoping that a large number of
clients will look through their collection in a short
time; clients attend knowing that they can see
a large range of work, from a variety of sources,
in a short timeframe. In return for charging the
agencies to exhibit, the fair organizers will actively
market the event to potential clients (it also
charges them to enter).

'Design is a plan for arranging
elements in such a way as best
to accomplish a particular
purpose.'

Charles Eames

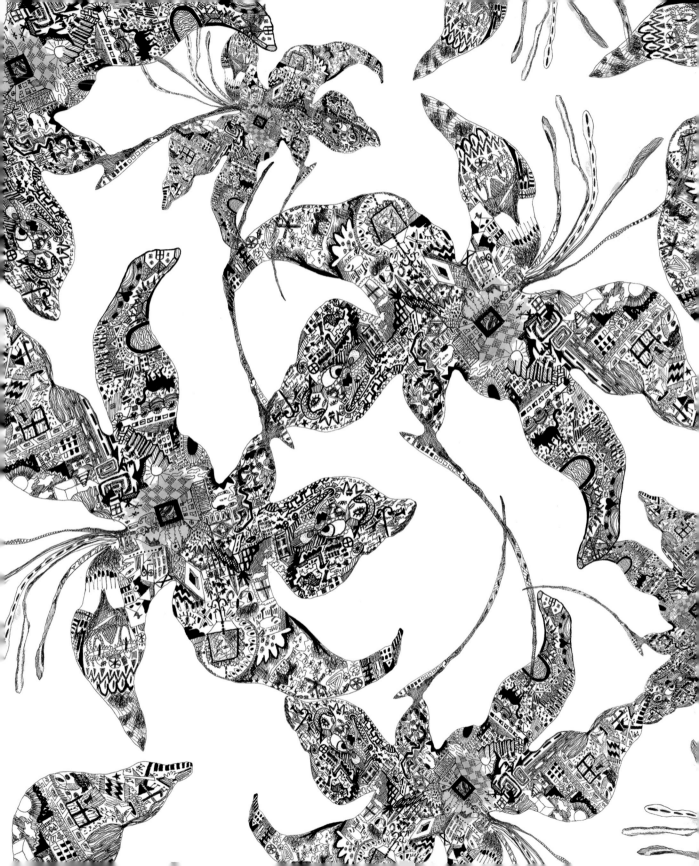

Chapter summary

As a printed textile practitioner, you answer briefs to create designs. These designs form collections, each targeted at a definite or suggested end-use, and linked by colour, content and style. The best of your collections form your portfolio, a body of work that demonstrates the full range of your design skills. The visual and verbal presentation of the portfolio should be underpinned by an awareness of what industry wants from it – speaking the right language with your presentation can open any number of doors.

It can be worth remembering that every established designer was once in the situation of nervously touting their portfolio round trying to get work. You must have the work that shows you can do the job, but you must also get it on the right desk. Talent will out, but you need to point it in the right direction.

Questions in summary

1. What factors link a series of designs together as a collection?
2. How does a printed textile designer start a collection?
3. What are the ingredients of a good portfolio?
4. How should the individual designs within a portfolio be presented?
5. What steps can a printed textile designer take to help break into the industry?
6. In what ways do the roles of employed designer and freelancer differ?

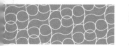

Technical considerations

The final chapter of this book looks at the practical and technical issues that printed textile designers need to be aware of. This breaks down into three sections:

The first is looking at what practitioners need to know in order to be able to design for manufacture. Once a print or pattern has been completed, it then has to go through a number of steps to get it onto cloth or whatever other substrate is being used. The work of a professional designer demonstrates an understanding of this, and to get you started, you should develop sufficient awareness to be able to do this too.

Secondly, a few guidelines are given on the design equipment you might need and how a bit of thought about your workspace and how you work in it can have an impact on the design process. A basic introduction to digital technology and formats is also given.

The final section looks at good working practice. These are the legal, health and safety and sustainable issues that form part of the framework within which professional designers work. In the case of legal and health and safety matters, this is information that you need to have an awareness of; with sustainability, your knowledge and ability to act creatively upon this could be an important part of your employability.

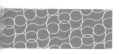

Designing for manufacture

It is almost impossible to underestimate how important a basic understanding of the manufacturing process is. Some of the requirements of print technology become so ingrained in professional designers that they become second nature – working with limited colour is one of the most obvious. However, it is possible to get overly concerned with how a design will physically be printed. If this involves any kind of mass production, it is highly likely that professional print designers will play no part in the process once their designs are signed off, with the possible exception of approving samples. A balance is required. The crucial thing is that you understand enough about print processes to ensure that your designs demonstrate that they can obviously be printed.

We are at a very interesting moment in printed textile design history, as the arrival of digital fabric printing may significantly alter the boundaries that practitioners have to work in. This is exciting stuff and you as a designer can help push the boundaries of what is possible. However, while screen printing remains the most common manufacturing technique, it is important for you to be aware of how to design for it.

Right:
A rotary screen printing machine. As the fabric passes under each rotary screen, the screen turns and coloured dyestuff is pushed through tiny holes in the screen from the inside. This transfers the design on the roller to the cloth. Each rotary screen on the machine corresponds to a separate colour.

Designing for screen printing

Although digital fabric printing is starting to become more commonplace, the vast majority of mass-produced printed textiles are manufactured using rotary screen printing. This process may be expensive to set up, but is still much faster and cheaper than the majority of digital fabric printing systems when printing in any quantity. Whilst this is the case, it will remain the dominant textile printing method, but its lifespan is limited. As digital printing costs drop and speeds increase, it is likely that this will replace screen printing as the mass production method of choice.

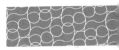

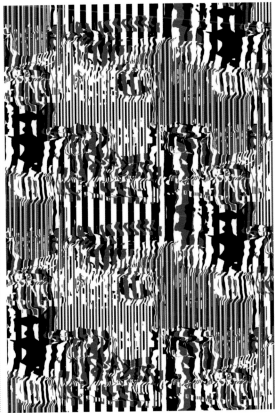

Whatever the future holds, the screen-print process is likely to remain important for a few years yet. If you want to work as a printed textile designer, this means you need sufficient knowledge of screen printing to be able to produce work for it. Of all the arguments for gaining practical experience of printing onto cloth, in day-to-day design terms, by far the most important thing to understand is how colour is applied to the fabric.

The screen-printing process normally requires each colour in a design to be printed separately. Thus, if a design features red, blue and yellow, each of these three colours will have its own screen. It is fairly common for the base colour of the fabric to be included in the design. Less common is overprinting, which involves deliberately printing one colour over a second to get a third. In the example used previously, red could be printed over yellow to get orange. The individual screens can print textured or flat areas of colour, or relatively fine detail, but cannot normally print tonal variations. If three different shades of the same blue are in a design, for instance, each will require its own screen. The more colours a design has, the more screens required to print it and the higher the production costs.

If the practitioner is required to produce the design in repeat (as is likely to be the case for most furnishing end-uses), then this needs to be both accurate and to the correct size. If you are designing in repeat and the brief does not give details of this, you should clarify everything immediately. Just as the colour palette is normally factored in from the very start, so is the repeat size and structure.

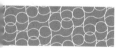

Opposite:
The smaller black and white images show the four colour separations for the large design. Files of images like these would be used to create the screens required to print the design.

Colour separations for screen printing

In design terms, the fact that every colour requires a different screen means that you need to be very aware of both which and how many colours to work with. This is one of the reasons why colour palettes are so important and why they will have been decided on very early in the design process. Working with traditional media, designers generally mix up, say, paint to each colour in the palette; practitioners working digitally will set up a range of colour swatches to use. This means they can get a good idea of how the design will print as they are working on it. Although it is possible to create a multi-colour design and then re-work it to limit the colours (this is actually quite easy with computers), it generally will end up looking very different, particularly if only a very limited colour palette is available.

Once a design has been signed off for printing, colour separations will be made from it. A separation is all the bits of a design that will be printed in a particular colour – so in theory, a two-colour design will have two separations: one for each colour. A three-colour design will have three and so on. In practice, if one of the colours is white (or the same colour as the fabric before it is printed), one less separation will be needed. The areas that are white (say) don't need to be printed; the base colour can be left as it is in the corresponding areas of the pattern. Sometimes the fabric is dyed first and then has colour printed onto it.

The separation process used to be done by hand (often by trainee textile designers). A special translucent drafting film, often referred to as Kodatrace, would be laid over the design, and all the areas of the first colour would be traced onto it using an opaque, gouache-like paint, generally known as Photopac. Another Kodatrace would then be placed on the design, onto which all the areas of the second colour would be painted and the same process would continue until all the colours were on separate films. These would then be used to create the screens for printing. Each film would also have registration marks traced very accurately off the original. These would be used to align the individual screens so there were no gaps or overlaps between each colour.

Clearly, doing separations by hand is a laborious process, and in industry the process is almost invariably now done digitally. If the design is not already digitized, it is scanned or photographed and software is used to create the separations for each colour. In some cases, designers might be asked to do this as part of the brief. Although the industry might use a specialist program to do this, it is perfectly possible with any widely used image-editing program such as Photoshop® or Illustrator®, although the process is made considerably easier if the design has been created with the final number of colours in mind from the start. The separations are then transferred to screen ready for printing. For rotary screens, this is generally done by digitally driven laser cutters, cutting meshes into thin nickel.

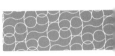

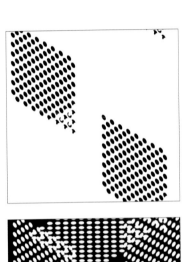

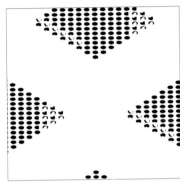

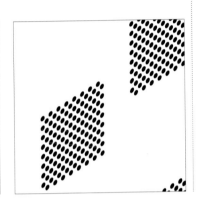

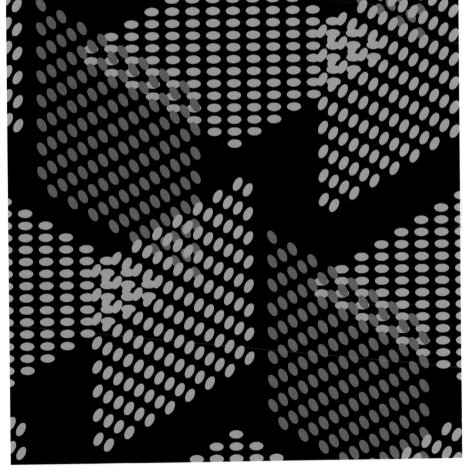

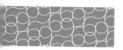

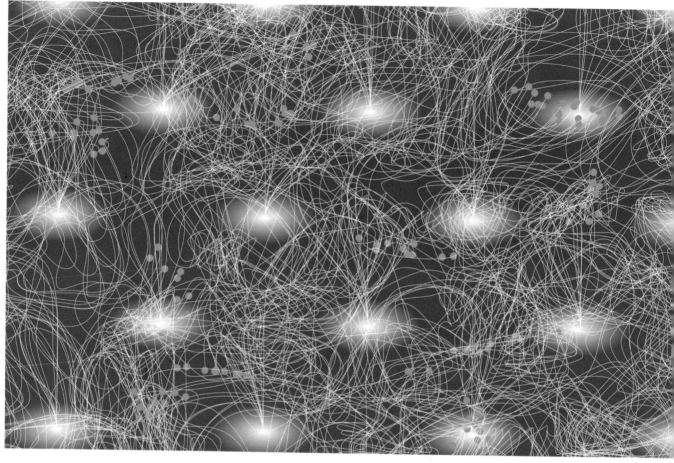

Above:
A design for digital print with a gradient – a shading effect from one colour to another that would be very difficult to achieve with earlier printing methods.

Colour separations for other fabric printing processes

There are pockets of industry that use technologies to print other than screen or digital processes. Designers working in the wallpaper industry, for example, may find themselves creating print and pattern for roller printing. Such a process follows the same principles as rotary screens. As each colour will require a different (say) roller or block, all the elements of the design in that colour need to be separated out and cut into the printing surface. The exception to this is transfer printing, where an automatic CMYK separation process may be used.

Designing for digital printing

Digital fabric printing provides the opportunity for a fundamental shift in the possibilities of printed textile design. History would suggest that designers and manufacturers will have very different approaches to the use of this new technology; it suggests that designers will want to experiment and develop new ways of designing, whilst manufacturers will take a more cautious approach, mindful that many design staples have remained popular through changes from block to roller to screen-printing techniques.

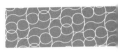

Digital printing onto fabric eliminates the need for separations. The design is essentially sent straight to the printer and can be any number of colours. The same process applies to other types of printing that are normally controlled digitally. An example of this is the offset litho process used for giftwrap or cards. The designer may have to identify any spot colours.

As has already been explored on pages 52-77, digital printing may have an effect on the design of printed textiles, as it has the potential to free practitioners from working with limited colour palettes and conventional repeat. It does currently have limitations, however – of the range of printing methods listed on the previous pages, only dyestuffs and pigments are currently widely digitally printed. Furthermore, getting good depth of colour on heavyweight fabrics is difficult. Whilst it is likely that the new technology will develop to give a greater range of printing methods (and probably some new ones), so will it affect the way printed textile designers work. Digital fabric printing offers new freedoms, but also new constraints.

In practical terms, designing for digital print normally involves saving the final design in a particular file format (typically .TIF) and with a particular colour mode (generally LAB), although any necessary conversions can be carried out by the printers. As with any print process, if the designer is asked to produce the design in repeat, it should be accurate and the correct size (normally at 300dpi). Digital printers put a design into repeat by tiling it over the surface of the fabric. If the top of the design doesn't match the bottom, the printer won't magically correct it - it remains up to the designer to get it right beforehand.

Exploiting the new technology

Probably the most fundamental change that digital fabric printing initially offers is unlimited colour palettes. It is possible to print a design that has millions of different colours for the first time. From a manufacturing standpoint, the cost of the print varies very little regardless of the number of colours involved. This is such a seismic change in the way textile printing on a large scale has ever operated before that it will take some time for both designers and customers to react.

Allied to this is the ease with which photographic imagery blends from one colour to another. Both have been possible before; transfer printing, for example, makes both feasible. However, the range of fabric it can be printed onto is limited and it requires completely different printing equipment from (say) rotary screens. Digital printers offer the possibility of printing almost any image onto almost any fabric.

The ease of this may be a bit of a mixed blessing. Just because it is possible to put any image onto fabric doesn't mean any image looks good there. Although the technology may be changing, the qualities that make pattern good remain largely unchanged.

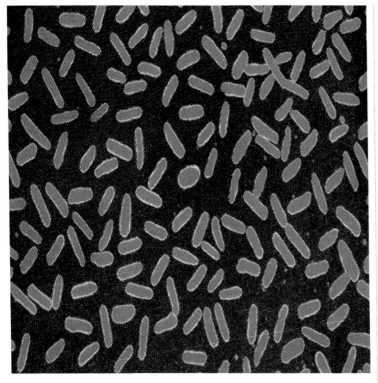

Above:
Discharge fabric
sample – the black
has been bleached
out with the
discharge; the pink
is an illuminating
dye, resistant to the
bleach it was mixed
in with.

Designing for other print methods

Other printing methods that pattern designers may
create work for essentially fall into two categories:
those that require limited colour palettes and
those that do not. The former normally involve
some form of separation. Pattern designers working
for giftware, for example, where the surface is
paper, are likely to have their designs printed by
an off-set litho process and have no restriction
in palette. The same may apply to transfer prints,
which are printed onto paper before being heat
pressed onto fabric. It should be noted, however,
that such a print process may involve a set number
of spot colours rather than the optical mixing of
standard CMYK printing.

Print processes for fabric

There are a wide variety of different dyes or
inks that can be used to apply colour to fabric.
By far the most commonly used are either dyes
or pigments, but there are a number of other
processes that may be used. It is possible to
combine different print processes, but this is fairly
uncommon in industry, probably due to the high
production costs involved. It should also be noted
that printing is not the only method by which
to pattern fabric – construction techniques such
as jacquard weaving or carpet tufting may also
be used, as may other embellishment techniques
such as embroidery. The following list covers the
main methods of applying print colour.

Dyes

The most common category, dyestuffs react
chemically with the fabric to change it to the
desired colour. Dyestuff will not affect the handle
of the fabric, or alter its surface quality. They
are normally transparent – a blue printed onto
yellow base fabric would come out green. The
choice of the dyestuff tends to be governed by
the fabric it is being printed onto. Reactive dyes,
for example, work best on cellulose or cellulistic
fibres such as cotton, linen or viscose. Acid dyes
are commonly used for protein fabrics such as
silk or wool, but may be used on nylon. Disperse
dyes are commonly used on polyester. In screen
printing, all the chemicals required are mixed in
with the print paste; in digital printing, the fabric
is pre-treated with all the required ingredients
except the actual dye, which goes on as the fabric
runs through the printer. In either case, the cloth
is then steamed or baked to fix the colour, and
then washed thoroughly. Disperse dyes can also
be transferred to the fabric from pre-printed paper
via heated metal plates or rollers. Although some
dyes will fade with repeated washing or exposure
to light, they tend to have a good lifespan.

Pigments

This process physically attaches colour to the fabric as a layer that coats the surface. Depending on the pigment used, this can have an effect on the surface quality of the fabric and on the way it handles. Pigments can be applied to any fabric that will withstand the fixing process, which generally involves heat, although some are cured by special light sources (infra-red, for example) and others require no fixing at all. They can be transparent or opaque, the latter able to cover any base colour of fabric. Some pigments may not be as permanent as dyes; in particular they may be susceptible to surface abrasion or fabric stretching. Pigments can be applied by screen or digital printing. Metallic, pearlescent or other effects are possible that cannot be achieved with dyestuffs.

Discharge

This is most commonly a dye process, although a pigment version is occasionally used. The fabric to be printed is pre-dyed with a bleachable base colour. The discharge paste, which contains a bleaching agent, is printed onto it, normally with screens. When it is steamed, the discharge reacts with the base fabric colour, bleaching it out. Dye that is resistant to the bleach (known as illuminating colour) can be added to the discharge paste. The base colour is bleached out and the illuminating colour replaces it.

Foiling and flocking

The fabric is screen printed with a glue. With foiling, a metallic foil is then applied to the fabric (normally with heat), only sticking to the glued areas. This gives a greater degree of shine than is possible with metallic pigments. The flocking process scatters tiny fibres across the fabric, which are charged electrically to make them stand up. They only stick to the glued areas. Both can be applied to most fabrics, but are not particularly hard wearing and have a considerable effect on fabric handle.

Devoré or burn out

A highly acidic paste is screen printed onto a specially constructed fabric. Cellulose or cellulostic yarns such as cotton, linen or viscose are eaten away, protein (wool or silk) or synthetic yarns (polyester or nylon) remain. In general, the fabric is woven or knitted so that eating the (say) cotton away leaves (say) polyester sections, rather than burning holes on the fabric.

Puff

A type of pigment that expands on warming. The puff binder, possibly mixed with pigment colour, is screen printed onto the fabric and then heated, giving a raised, slightly rubbery print. It is not particularly hard wearing. Puff can sometimes be printed onto the reverse of stretch fabrics to give a textured, 3D effect.

Laser cutting

Technically not a print process, this may be used to cut a design out of a fabric or to remove a thin layer of fabric from the surface, etching the pattern into the cloth.

Left:
Tord Boontje's 'Serre' design for Kvadrat features the devoré technique.

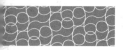

Equipment list

Opposite:
It is worth thinking very carefully about your workspace set-up as it will have a considerable impact on the way you actually design.

Whatever the circumstances of your average day – whether you are employed, freelance or a student – you will work in a space and use a range of equipment. Even if you cannot control every aspect of these things, optimizing your resources is a very important part of the design process.

This section will look at the kit that most practitioners are likely to find themselves working with and how to make the most of the environment in which you design. How you organize these things can have a big effect on both the quality and efficiency of your working life and it is worth spending some time to get them right.

Setting up a workspace

How you set out the space you work in can have a considerable effect on your working process. Regardless of whether you are working in a corner of a room at home, in an office-style environment for an employer or in your own studio space, giving a bit of thought to your immediate environment can help you work smarter. How you do this normally boils down to thinking about the equipment you use and the resources you need to refer to in order to answer the brief you're working on. If you spend a significant amount of time getting all your drawing and painting equipment out of a drawer every day, would you be better leaving everything out so you can get started straight away? If your desk gets cluttered with inspirational imagery, would it be better to have it all pinned or taped up on a wall?

Some designers like to have their working environment very neat and tidy, with everything in its place. Others prefer a more chaotic approach, with inspirational imagery and design materials scattered freely about their workspace. In practice, most designers operate somewhere between the two extremes. It really doesn't matter where this point is for you, just that you recognize when you've got the balance right. If you spend more time tidying up than designing, you should probably think about trying to take a more relaxed approach. If you spend hours every day looking for where you put the work you did last week, it is likely that you need to be a bit more organized.

Ideally, your working environment should reflect the different techniques and media you are likely to use on a regular basis. If you use a mix of hand drawing/painting and digital processes, then you should try to set up a space for both. In practice, you may not have room to do this, but you can still think about ways to quickly switch between the two.

As well as thinking about the space you work in, it is also a good idea to think about how you work. This is essentially about becoming aware of what you need to do to operate efficiently. Collecting inspirational imagery, for example, but spending hours categorizing it alphabetically into a file that you never open again is pointless. Although shoving it all randomly in a box may initially appear unorganized, the process of digging through the box to find something may mean you chance upon other inspirational imagery that you had forgotten about.

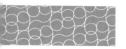

Above:
No matter how digitally complex working methods become, many designers still rely on basic painting and drawing equipment to sketch out and develop their ideas.

Developing workflow

Even when faced with a tight deadline, reflection is a crucial part of the design process. How you develop your workflow should not purely revolve around efficiency; quality is fundamental. Most designers will have experienced the situation of spending a long time tinkering with a small element of a design, unable to decide exactly how to get it right. Having a break, or working on something else for a bit very often provides the perspective to decide how best to solve the problem.

This will also be framed by the requirements of your client or employer - it's no good claiming that you cannot be creative before 3pm if you are working a 9 to 5 day. Optimizing your workflow should be about improvement, not self indulgence.

It is true that you have to put a lot of hours in if you want to get good. Most people in the creative industries work very hard, but are far more likely to enjoy their work than many other professions. However, it is important to strike a work/life balance. Spending a lot of time doing something doesn't automatically make it better than something that took ten minutes. Recognizing that the way you organize and reflect on your work has a big effect on the quality of your designs is a vital part of becoming a good designer, but also a happy one who has a life outside work.

'There are three principal means of acquiring knowledge... observation of nature, reflection, and experimentation.'

Denis Diderot

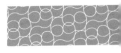

General painting and drawing

Although printed textile design is becoming increasingly digital, most practitioners still use a range of traditional media. Even the most resolutely digital of practitioners may be glad from time to time that you don't have to wait five minutes for a pencil to boot up. Equally, spending hours creating a brush mark using software may be a rather laborious process in comparison to doing a bit of mark making and scanning. Exactly what media you use will depend to a large degree on the individual and the circumstances of your work. Most designers develop a fairly clear understanding of the particular media for which they have an affinity during their education, but it is always worth trying out new techniques and processes. This can be particularly valuable if you feel your work is in a rut. It is important to appreciate that patience may be required to do this, and that it is likely to be what you do with the technique, rather than the technique itself, that matters.

Traditionally, for many textile designers, the last stage of the design process was done in gouache, applying paint mixed up in advance to the palette onto designs planned out in pencil on paper or sometime acetate. In the hands of a skilled practitioner, gouache gives smooth flat colour that makes it easy to see how a design will translate into print. However, designers have always used a range of other media and it is fine to experiment with any you like, provided you can successfully answer the brief. In the past, the use of some media might have been limited by the range of colours available – a particular type of marker pen, for example, may only be available in a limited range of hues. Now that traditional media can be scanned and re-coloured digitally, this is no longer an issue.

Above:
Although hands-on screen printing experience isn't vital to a career in printed textile design, it is important to have an understanding of how the print process works and the impact this has on the design process.

The importance of drawing

The difficulty of mastering the use of any media is important. The irregular scratching of a traditional ink pen or the infinite variety of mark and shading that can be obtained with a very soft pencil require a lot of practice to gain confidence in using. Once these facilities have been obtained, however, they are likely to form a cornerstone of the designer's skill base, even if they only form part of a design process that ultimately ends digitally (for printed textile designers, digital is probably the new gouache). Printed textile designers are employed by industry because of their abilities to translate briefs via creative use of media into visual information that can act as instructions to a manufacturer. It seems such an obvious thing to say, but this requires skill in drawing and using colour, and learning those skills is a huge stride towards professional success.

Screen printing

Until relatively recently, most printed textiles design programmes included at least some training in screen printing. Not all art and design colleges and faculties have been able to retain this provision, often because the large space required to house print tables is seen as inefficient and costly by the larger institution they are part of. Some freelance designer studios do print their designs on fabric (although this is often the job of the juniors) and some designers who work for a printing company or converters may also use the technology. Provided you understand how the print process works and the impact this has on the design process, having limited hands-on screen printing experience needn't adversely affect a career.

Hardware overview

Hardware is digital equipment that physically exists. Computers, printers, scanners and digital cameras are all hardware. The computer itself is clearly at the heart of everything else; other hardware may be referred to as peripherals.

If you are employed as a designer, it is likely that you will have a computer provided for you. Whilst some areas of design are entirely Mac based, printed textile practitioners are more likely than (say) graphic designers to use PCs. You should not assume that just because you have used a Mac throughout your studies that an employer will do the same. Whichever operating system you use or prefer, make sure you have a working knowledge of how to work the other – once you're actually using the software, there is very often remarkably little difference. If you are a freelance designer or a student, you will almost certainly have to buy one. Arguments about whether PCs or Macs are better tend to get very tedious very quickly and it is not the place of this book to recommend one over the other. If you're using software like Adobe® Creative Suite® that operates almost identically over the two operating systems, the argument is largely irrelevant and it ultimately comes down to personal preference. In either case, always make sure that what you are buying is powerful enough to deal with the software you are going to run on it. Similarly, it's up to you whether you would rather have a laptop or a desktop – the latter are cheaper, but can be less convenient. If you are working on a laptop for long periods of time at the same desk, to avoid risk of RSI (Repetitive Strain Injury) or back problems, you should get a proper keyboard and mouse to plug into it and a stand to put it on.

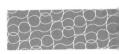

Backing up your work on a regular basis is absolutely vital. It's not a case of if the hard drive in your computer fails, it's a question of when. Data recovery may be possible, but it can take time and be very costly. Get an external hard drive and back your work up regularly. There's never a good time for hard drives to fail, but you should work on the basis that you can deal with it occurring just before a deadline. At the very least, back up every week.

How much additional hardware you need to buy will depend on your circumstances. If you are employed, you may have everything provided, but freelancers will probably need to budget for a camera, a scanner and a printer. Investing in an A3+ (tabloid+) printer is probably worthwhile. Some designers do have large-format printers, but it is probably best to see if you really need one before investing, as purchase costs rise exponentially with size.

One additional piece of hardware that is definitely worth considering is a graphics tablet. They make image editing far easier than working with a mouse or touch / trackpad, particularly when working with vector-based software. They are much more accurate than mice or touchpads but more natural as well - drawing feels like drawing. The most common brand in professional use is Wacom.

Software overview

Software is the programs that your computer hardware runs. You tell the software's interface what you want it to do and the software then uses the hardware to carry out your instructions.

It is very important to factor in software costs when budgeting for a digital set-up. Professional software is not cheap and it is no use blowing all your money on hardware if you can't afford to buy the software you need in order to do your design work. In many cases you can save money by buying a package of software; this can be much cheaper than buying the programs individually. If you are a student, make the most of being able to get very substantial discounts on software.

Although there are a number of different design programs on the market, the most common two in use by printed textile designers are Adobe® Photoshop® and Illustrator®. Whilst there are specialist textile design software packages available, these are the two that are increasingly likely to be mentioned in job specifications. Investing in a textile specific package in case it is mentioned in a job advert is a gamble, and it probably isn't worth buying one unless you are freelancing and are convinced it will improve your workflow (this is rare). Equally, there are other, less expensive (or even free) image-editing programs out there, but you may find yourself somewhat isolated in using them.

'You can't do better design with a computer, but you can speed up your work enormously.'

Wim Crouwel

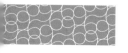

Pixels and paths

Image-editing software normally works in one of two ways. Raster or bitmap systems divide the image up into squares of colour called pixels. Vector or line art systems divide an image up into a series of shapes that are defined by a line (known as a path) around the edge of them.

Raster-based software is good at dealing with photographs or other complex imagery. For most people, the programs are more intuitive and tend to be easier to learn. Large raster images have large file sizes and may require powerful computers to edit them – less potent machines may take an age to perform some tasks, or not be able to deal with them at all. Images made up of pixels do not enlarge well – in general going anything bigger than double the original size will result in noticeable blurring or evidence of the original pixelation.

Vector-based software is generally better for more graphic elements or type. Images created from paths can be enlarged to any size with no loss of quality and tend to have far smaller file sizes than their raster equivalents. Elements of images can be very easily edited – lines can be re-shaped, for example, without needing to change any other part of the image. However, learning how to use the software normally involves a steep learning curve and it can take some while to really be able to push the boundaries of what it can do. Although photographic imagery can be converted to paths, the image will significantly change in doing so; unless such an effect is desired, photos are almost never edited in vector-based programs.

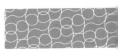

File formats

When you are working on a digital brief, it is always very important to establish what format the final designs should be in. Whilst it is possible to change the format of a file at any time (usually via the Save As function most software has), this may be problematic.

If a client asks for a design in a vector-based file format, for example, it would be possible to create the work in a pixel-based program, then open it in (say) Illustrator® and save it in a path-based format such as .EPS or .AI. However, the content of the image itself would still be pixels. For a client to make the request, it is likely that they want the scalability and editability of vectors – the content of the image needs to be in paths. Although the image you have created is technically in the correct format, it is probably unable to be used in the way they had intended. It is possible to convert pixel-based content to paths via Illustrator's® Live Trace function, but this is likely to significantly alter the image unless it was very graphic to start with.

Some pixel-based formats reduce file size by a process known as compression. In some cases, such as LZW in the .TIF format, this doesn't make the image appear any different – this is lossless compression. Other methods, such as the .JPG format, change the image to get the drop in file size – lossy compression. Once this has happened, the missing visual information cannot be got back. Repeatedly editing and resaving an image in such a format will gradually degrade it.

It is important to keep an eye on two things here. First, establish from the outset which format the brief requires and why it should be in that format. Secondly, only flatten or compress images if specifically told to do so (to e-mail a design idea, for example) and always keep the original, fully editable version.

Left:
Vector image editing software divides an image up into coloured lines or shapes, saving points along the paths that map them out.

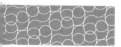

Good working practice

As with most professional careers, the work of a printed textile designer is often bound by contracts or other forms of written agreement. These are to safeguard both designer and client or employer. Having an awareness of what is involved is important as it will form part of the process of getting a job, even if your part in this is simply to read a contract and check you understand and agree with its contents before you sign it.

Equally, you should be aware of your health and safety at work, something that many freelancers ignore. A lot of this is common sense – if you know you are going to spend a significant proportion of your working life staring at a computer monitor, for instance, having your desk and chair set up to minimize any risk of long-term back problems needs to be taken into consideration.

It is also important to think about the steps you can take to make your practice sustainable – if you don't think industry is doing enough, you should lead by example. These elements of good working practice will be considered in this section.

Copyright

Copyright is essentially the entitlement to use a design, normally for commercial purposes. If you are employed, your contract will probably state that the copyright of all the design work you do is owned by your employer. If you are working freelance, you automatically own the copyright to a design you create; with printed textile design, this normally transfers to the client when you sell it. If you are working to commission and have a contract with your client, it may state that they own the rights to everything you create for them, including all development work or unused designs. You can of course keep a copy for your own records (the contract will usually state this), but once a design is sold, you should not use it or any elements from it in any other work. Furthermore, unless you have permission from the new copyright holder, you should not show it publicly (on a website, for example) unless you have their written permission.

Never attempt to pass off anyone else's work in any form as your own. It doesn't matter if it is part of a famous existing design or something you found on page 8 of your Google® Images search – unless you have written permission from the copyright holder to use it, don't.

Left:
Unless you have express permission to use other people's imagery, always make sure every element of a design is created by you. You can use as many different media as the brief allows to do this – just make sure it's all original.

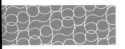
Licensing

Relatively rare in print and pattern design in relation to other fields of design such as illustration, licensing is the sale of a design for a specific use or length of time (often both). The practitioner retains the copyright, but the client buys the right to use the work. Once it has been used for that purpose, or the time period has elapsed, the designer is then free to offer the design's licence for sale again, potentially to the same client. In practice, the brief involved is quite likely to mean that the design is unlikely to be suitable for another client, but the designer would be free to use the work for publicity purposes, for example, unlike a design where the copyright has been signed over in perpetuity.

Contracts

Almost every employer will ask you to sign a contract before you work for them; if you are represented by an agency, it is likely you will do the same. Freelancers may also be asked to sign them when working on a particular job. You should read them carefully before you sign and never let yourself feel pressured to sign – you should be given the time to go through them carefully and discuss any issues you have. By signing it, you are agreeing to it – if something goes wrong down the line, ignorance of its contents will be no defence.

Non-disclosure or confidentiality agreements

Because it can take such a long time to get a product to market once it has the input of a print and pattern practitioner, many companies are understandably keen that the designer involved doesn't run around telling everyone what it will look like before it is actually on sale (particularly their competitors). Non-disclosure (not telling people outside the company what they are working on), is a common part of employment contracts and may form part of the agreement with freelance commission work. Read the agreement carefully and discuss any concerns you have with the employer or client before you agree to the conditions.

In some cases, employment contracts may state that if you get a new job with a competitor, you are required to leave their offices immediately. In such cases you are normally paid for the notice term, but are not allowed to continue working for it (it may be jokingly referred to as gardening leave), but you should check this when you sign the contract.

As a freelancer, you can work for whoever offers you work, but you should still be very careful about what you show potential new clients. Showing them work you have done for another client might break both copyright and non-disclosure agreements. Not only that, but they may get the impression you will show any work you do for them to other people and be put off using you. Name dropping past clients is often a good idea (it helps convince a client you have the experience to deal with their job), but don't show the work you did for them unless you have their written permission, and tell the new client you're showing the work to that this is the case.

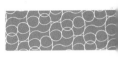

Terms and conditions

If you are working as a freelance designer, your terms and conditions are essentially a contract that your client must abide by. This would normally be stated on your invoice, but should be discussed before the work is started. Typically this happens at the moment the price is being negotiated. The T and Cs (as they may be referred to) might include details of how payment should be made – a month after invoicing is fairly standard, but you may require a percentage paid up front before the work is started, or charge additional costs for materials. In an attempt to prevent late payments by clients, an increasing number of agencies and designs stipulate that copyright or licensing rights do not pass to the client until payment has been received. The terms and conditions normally also state the agreed copyright or licensing agreement. This could vary from ownership of the copyright in perpetuity for~any use the client wants to a licence to use a design for a finite time period on a single product (the former is far more common). In some cases (particularly when working to commission), T and Cs may also stipulate that some payment has to be made even if the client doesn't ultimately accept the designs, or agree that once the client has signed the work off, any further changes will be chargeable.

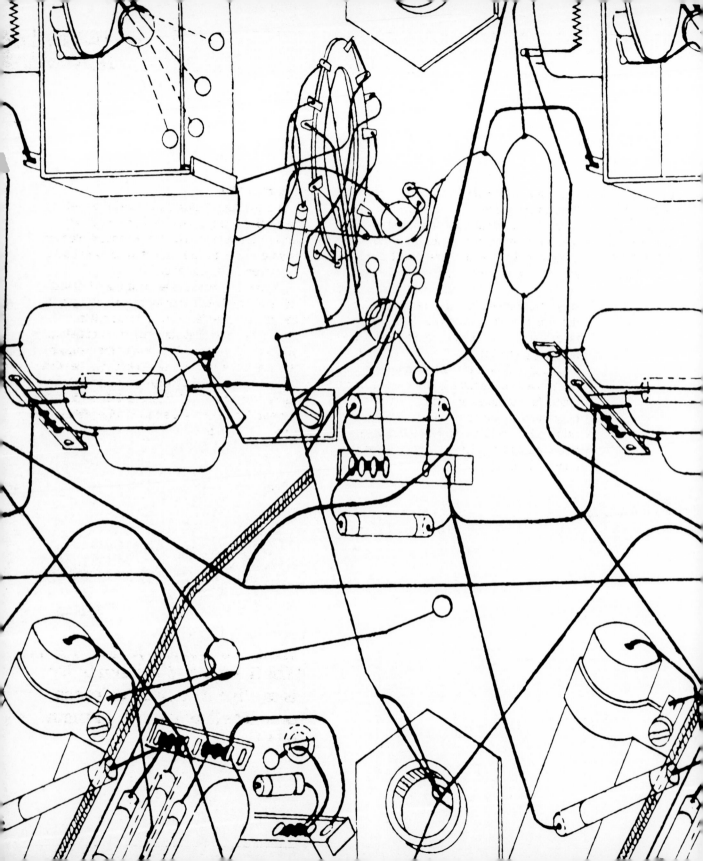

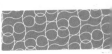

Occupational health and safety

If you are employed, your employer will be responsible for your health and safety at work. In practical terms for a designer, this means that your computer, design and chair should be correctly set up for your proportions. The temperature and lighting of your workspace, for example, are also subject to guidelines. If you are working freelance, the responsibility is up to you. It is important to take this seriously – simple things like getting the height of your chair right can have a big effect on long-term well-being. Because financial outlay can be involved – correctly adjustable and supportive chairs, for example, can be expensive – it can be easy for practitioners setting up a new practice to skimp on budgeting to look after themselves. It is important as it can have a dramatic effect on your quality of life as you get older.

Sustainability

Just as it is important to be aware of the legal issues that can help protect your work and to ensure that your own wellbeing is accounted for in your practice, so is it important to consider its impact on the environment.

If you care about sustainability and feel that the industry should be doing more to safeguard the future of the planet and its people, it is important to consider your own practice before you complain about others. Whilst the changes that you make may be tiny in relation to the whole, incremental positive change is still a good thing. As was suggested in Chapter one, this is a complex issue and some decisions may involve picking the lesser of two evils.

'The first rule of sustainability is to align with natural forces, or at least not try to defy them.'

Paul Hawken

Above:
Peter Ingwersen's Illuminati II project supplies organic and fair trade Ugandan cotton of the highest quality to the fashion industry.

Opposite:
Gossypium strive for ethical best practice across five areas: responsibility, sustainability, transparency, agriculture and textile processing.

Sustainability issues

As a student or a professional designer, part of your practice is being a consumer. You (or your company) have to buy materials, equipment and other resources in order to make your work. These resources include power, travel (even if it's just getting to work or college) You can't control all of these, but the ones that you can should be the ones you act on with regard to sustainability.

You should think about all the equipment you use on a daily basis. Does your paper come from sustainable sources and do you recycle all of it that you don't want to keep? Energy consumption is another example – not only does trying to minimize this save the earth's resources, it also saves on your bills. If the lifespan of your computer is about two years, and during this time it is running all day, every working day, clearly looking at power consumption should be an important factor in deciding which model to buy. At the end of its working life, don't just throw it out so it ends up in landfill. If you can't sell it or pass it on to someone else, at least recycle it.

Whilst it is important to have a good understanding of the issues involved, it could be argued that most people are now aware of the problem. They know that our actions are having a detrimental effect on the planet and that industry has treated some of its workforce badly for a long time. Awareness is an important thing, but it is only the first step.

Somehow, sustainability has to be embedded in the textiles industry. Regardless of whether a consumer is aware that a particular product is sustainable, industry, and by extension designers, have to find a way of making it more desirable than one that isn't. Even more problematically, people need to be encouraged to consume less – the desirability has to be about need, rather than want. Trying to work out how to do this is one of the big challenges of the twenty-first century. The creative abilities of designers ought to be at the heart of this; your own practice should be the start.

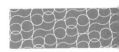

Chapter summary

As a designer, you will work with a range of media and equipment on a daily basis. Reflecting on what you use to create designs helps both to make you work better and ensure your client or employer's brief is answered.

As well as having the right technical awareness to physically make the designs, you also need to be aware of how they will be manufactured. Whilst you may not actually be working on fabric to do this, your design work should be able to reflect that you understand the process involved.

Part of being a good designer is having an understanding of the (say) manufacturing factors affecting your work, but there are other issues it is important to be aware of. Clearly these things are not the sole preserve of printed textile designers; nonetheless, it is important that you know about issues such as copyright and confidentiality, alongside health and safety.

Questions in summary

1. What processes are used to manufacture products featuring print and pattern?

2. Why is it important for printed textile designers to be aware of the manufacturing process?

3. Why is it worthwhile to think about the space you work in and the process you go through to create designs?

4. What equipment would a printed textile designer typically need to work with?

5. What professional practice issues must you be aware of before embarking on a career in printed textile design?

6. What responsibilities do print and pattern practitioners have to themselves and their environment?

Conclusion

As a professional printed textile designer, you need to have a set of skills that mean you can answer briefs. Answering a twenty-first-century brief well involves combining traditional abilities of drawing and colour use with digital techniques. Exactly which media or processes are involved will depend on the job, but being skilled in a good range of different methods and techniques is important. However, this is the means and not the end. It is what the designer does with the process, not the process itself, that makes the design demonstrate qualities such as originality, innovation or sophistication.

You need to understand the contexts within which you work. How good a designer you are (or think you are) means nothing if you can't communicate this. You must understand what the world you are trying to break into wants and your work should show you appreciate this. There is a big industry out there and it needs new ideas and talent all the time. However, it needs people who speak its language.

The difference between a professional designer and a student starting out on a new course boils down to experience - the professional will have spent thousands of hours getting both good and efficient at successfully creating work in response to a brief. Typically, they will be able to design in a range of different styles and do so very quickly, often appearing to spend very little time researching and even less developing their ideas before producing the final collection. These two skills - adaptability and the ability to quickly turn a project round - are generally cited by industry as the two things missing from graduates and their portfolios.

This book will not make you a good designer. It is a very general introduction to contemporary practice in printed textile design, intended to give a brief overview of the basic things you need to know about to get started on a career as a print and pattern designer. You will make you a good designer. You need to invest time both in learning the skills and being able to apply them to answer briefs. You also need to know about many different types of context: outcome or product, visual culture, manufacturing requirements, technological change, how industry operates and so on. Finally, you need to be able to communicate all this and demonstrate that you have both the skills and the contextual awareness. The reward for all this hard work is a deeply creative, challenging and satisfying career and the thrill of seeing your print and pattern enriching other people's lives.

Bibliography

Black, Sandy (ed.), Fashioning Fabrics, Black Dog Publishing, London, 2006.

Blackley, Lachlan, Wallpaper, Laurence King Publishing, London, 2006.

Bowie Style (Perkins, Marie), Print and Pattern, Laurence King Publishing, London, 2010.

Bowles, Melanie; Isaac, Ceri, Digital Textile Design, Laurence King Publishing, London, 2009.

Brown, Carol, Fashion and Textiles – The Essential Careers Guide, Laurence King Publishing, London, 2010.

Cole, Drusilla (ed.), 1000 Patterns, A and C Black, London, 2003.

Cole, Drusilla, Patterns – New Surface Design, Laurence King Publishing, London, 2007.

Dawber, Martin, New Fashion Print, Batsford, London, 2008.

Evans, Siân, Pattern Design – A Period Design Source Book, National Trust Books, London, 2008.

Fogg, Marnie, Print in Fashion, Batsford, London, 2006.

Glasner, Barbara; Schmidt, Petra; Schöndeling, Ursula (eds.), Patterns 2: Design, Art and Architecture, Birkhauser Verlag AG, Basel, 2007.

Joyce, Carol, Designing For Printed Textiles, Prentice-Hall Inc., Englewood Cliffs, 1982.

Meller, Susan; Elffers, Joost, Textile Designs, Thames and Hudson Ltd, London, 1991.

Parvathi, K., Textile Designing, Aavishkar Publishers, Jaipur, 2007.

Perry, Michael, Over and Over: A Catalog of Hand-Drawn Patterns, Princeton Architectural Press, New York, 2008.

Phillips, Peter; Bunce, Gillian, Repeat Patterns, Thames and Hudson Ltd, London, 1993.

Quinn, Bradley, Textile Designers at the Cutting Edge, Laurence King Publishing, London, 2009.

Schmidt, Petra; Tietenberg, Annette; Wollheim, Ralf (eds.), Patterns in Design, Art and Architecture, Birkhauser Verlag AG, Basel, 2007.

Schoeser, Mary, World Textiles – A Concise History, Thames and Hudson, London, 2003.

Seivewright, Simon, Basics Fashion Design: Research and Design, AVA Academica SA, Lausanne, 2007.

Sorger, Richard; Udale, Jenny, The Fundamentals of Fashion Design, AVA Academica SA, Lausanne, 2006.

Storey, Joyce, Textile Printing, Thames and Hudson Ltd, London, 1974.

Tain, Linda, Portfolio Presentation for Fashion Designers, Fairchild Publications, Inc., New York, 2003.

Udale, Jenny, Basics Fashion Design: Textiles and Fashion, AVA Academica SA, Lausanne, 2008.

Ujiie, Hitoshi, Digital Printing of Textiles, Woodhead Publishing Ltd, Cambridge, 2006.

Valli, Marc-A (ed.), Graphic Magazine Issue Eight: Ornate!, BIS Publishers, Amsterdam, 2005.

Viction: Workshop (ed.), Fashion Unfolding, Viction:workshop Ltd., Hong Kong, 2007.

Viction: Workshop (ed.), Simply Pattern, Viction:workshop Ltd., Hong Kong, 2008.

Waddell, Gavin, How Fashion Works, Blackwell Publishing, Oxford, 2004.

Glossary

Baking – commonly used fixing process for printed textiles, involving the application of dry heat to the fabric for a set length of time.

Batik – a wax resist process used to both print and dye fabric.

Blank – printed fabric samples sewn together to create what appears to be typically just the front of a fairly simple garment. Used by some studios to show their designs. The term front is also sometimes used.

Bleed – in textile printing, the undesired spread of colour during or after the print process, resulting in a blurred design. Normally caused by too many pulls, too thin a thickener or insufficient washing.

Block – either a type of repeat structure where the design tiles exactly horizontally and vertically over the substrate or a cut or inlaid stamp used in the block printing process or a template used to cut out part of a garment from fabric.

Coated fabric (also known as pre-treated fabric) – in the context of this book, a fabric that has been treated with a chemical to prepare it for digital printing. The chemical reacts with the dyestuff at the fixing stage to set the colour into the cloth.

Colour fastness – a durability of a dyestuff to washing, abrasion, light or any other factor that might alter it.

Colour forecast or prediction – a palette intended to provide an indication of what clients or customers may be interested in for a specific future season or point in time. Typically, this provides some context for its appeal and in some cases its end-use. Trends almost invariably include a colour forecast.

Colour separation – creating an image of each separate colour in a design, or dividing the image up into a set number of colours. Each separation is then used to create a screen, for example.

Colourway – an alternate version of a design with exactly the same content, but a different colour palette. The palette may be tonally similar to the original.

Computer aided manufacture – the use of digital technology in the manufacturing process.

Computer integrated manufacture – a design and production process in which all information (including visual) is digital. A design created with CAD can be directly printed by CAM, for example, but every other aspect of getting the product to the customer is also controlled by computers.

Conversion – the process of creating a finished fabric from its constituent fibres; this may include the print process. Companies that do this are called converters.

Copper plate printing – a design is etched or engraved into a flat copper surface. Colour is then applied to the plate, the surface of which immediately has the colour removed, leaving it only in the etched or engraved parts. The plate is then applied to the substrate and pressure is applied, transferring the design.

Copper roller printing – a mechanised version of copper plate printing. The copper surface is cylindrical; the roller turns as the substrate is passed over or under it with pressure. The colour is applied, the excess is removed and the design is printed onto the fabric as it turns.

Curing – a fixing process, normally involving time, heat or a specific type or light. The term is normally only used in the textile industry for certain types of pigment print.

Devoré – an acidic paste is printed onto a specially constructed fabric of two fibre types. When steamed or baked, the acid removes one fibre type, leaving the other as a more transparent pattern.

Digital fabric printing – a digitised design is printed onto fabric by spraying tiny drops of dyestuff or pigment onto its surface.

Discharge (printing) – a print process that removes existing colour from a fabric. The print paste can contain a dye resistant to the bleaching process called an illuminant which will re-colour the printed areas.

Fixing – after the dyestuff or pigment has been printed onto the fabric, in most cases the colour(s) have to be permanently set into or onto it. This is typically done by steaming or baking the fabric. The fabric is then washed to remove any excess colour and print paste.

Flat-bed screen printing – term used to differentiate printing with horizontal (flat) screens as opposed to rotary screen printing. In some cases, the term implies using the mechanised process, rather than printing by hand.

Flock (printing), flocking – the design is printed onto the substrate with glue. Tiny fibres are applied to the surface and stick to the glued areas, giving a velvet-like appearance. In some cases, an electrostatic charge is applied to the fibres to get them to all stand to lie in the same direction.

Greige (cloth or goods) - uncoloured (or unfinished) fabric or garments that are intended to be subsequently printed, dyed or finished in some way. Sometimes known as grey cloth or goods.

Header - a card strip running across the top of a sample or blank to support and display it. Headers may feature hooks or hangers to allow them to be displayed on a rail. The term hanger is occasionally used instead.

Ikat (dyeing) - a (normally resist) dyeing process where colour is applied to the vertical (warp) or horizontal (weft) yarn (or both) before it is woven.

Lithography - a print process that uses oil and water's repulsion of each other. Although never widely used in textile printing, offset lithography (litho) is commonly used to print on paper (such as stationery or gift-wrap) in large quantities.

Mordant - a substance that improves the strength of a dye's bond to the substrate.

Print paste - a combination of ingredients used by any print process used to carry the colour. Typically this will include dye or pigment, thickener and chemicals to physically or chemically attach the colour to the substrate.

Pull - in hand or flat-bed screen printing, each pass of the squeegee and print paste is a pull (regardless of the direction it is made in). A pull made without any print paste is a dry pull.

Raster image processor - specialist software used to set up and drive a digital (fabric) printer.

Registration marks or crosses - small crosses or similar symbols used to align each separate colour of a print. These are typically visible on the selvedge of a fabric.

Repeat - in order to cover a fabric or other substrate with pattern, the design is replicated down and (normally) across it. The structure of this replication is known as repeat.

Resist (printing) - a substance applied to certain areas of the substrate that acts as a barrier against subsequent dyeing or printing. When the resist is removed, those areas covered by it remain uncoloured.

Roller printing - a print process involving a roller with a design cut into it. Dyestuff is applied and as the substrate is passed over or under it, the pattern is transferred. Examples include copper roller printing and rubber roller printing.

Rotary screen printing - the design is cut as a mesh into a cylinder made from thin metal. The print paste is pumped into it and the substrate is moved under it so the cylinder rolls over it. A metal blade inside the cylinder pushes the colour through the holes in the mesh to print the design into it.

Silk screen (printing) - the mesh stretched over a screen is now almost always made of polyester, but used to be made of silk. The term remains in occasional use and has nothing to do with silk being a potential substrate.

Specification sheet, spec sheet - information resource used in the manufacture of a product. For the print process, this might involve dyestuff to be used, colour references, position of the print or any of a number of other factors.

Steaming - commonly used fixing process for printed textiles, involving the application of steam to the fabric for a set length of time.

Stencilling - holes are cut into (typically) paper or very thin metal and colour is applied through the holes to the surface below. The forerunner of screen printing.

Strike off - a sample used to approve the design, colour, repeat and registration of a printed textile.

Texture mapping - a CAD process that places a pattern (or any fabric texture) onto a virtual 3D product or end-use.

Tjanting - a pen-like tool used to draw lines of molten wax onto fabric in the batik process.

Tjap - a block used to stamp a design in molten wax onto fabric in the batik process.

Transfer printing - the design is printed into one substrate (paper or film, for example) and then transferred to another (such as fabric or a ceramic) via a process such as heat or pressure.

Width for length (printing) - after printing, the fabric is rotated through 90 degrees to make the product, so what was the fabric's sides become its top and bottom. Commonly used for large end-uses with borders such as duvet covers.

Index

Page numbers in *italics* refer to illustrations.

Compiled by Indexing Specialists (UK) Ltd

Acknowledgements & Picture credits

Acknowledgements

The author would like to thank the following people for their part in this book:

David and Tasie Russell, for nurturing my drawing and all their encouragement; Sophie Russell, for letting the cat out of the bag; Richard Daniel, for introducing me to printing in the first place; Alan Holmes, Dr. Annie Shaw and Julie Haslam, for making work a pleasure; all TD4Fers past and present, particularly Hannah Exall, Lucy O'Brien, Claire Roberts, Emmanuelle Sayers, Joasia Staszek, Abbey Watkins and Carmen Wood for allowing their work to be used; Frans Verschuren, for so many design opportunities; Philip Sykas, for help with photographing the designs from the Downing Collection; Leafy Robinson, for being a thoughtful and sympathetic editor; Ian Welch, for the picture research; Studio8 Design, for the layout and to all the designers whose print and pattern is featured. The publisher would also like to thank Tom Embleton, Anne Marie Howat and Jimmy Stephen-Cran for their help with reviewing various versions of the manuscript.

Finally, this would not have been possible without the love, patience and support of Jude Russell.

This book is for Jude and Joe.

Picture credits

p11 Image © V&A Images / Victoria & Albert Museum, London
p12 Image courtesy of the Downing Collection at Manchester School of Art
p14 Image © V&A Images / Victoria & Albert Museum, London
p15 Copyright unknown
p16 Image © V&A Images / Victoria & Albert Museum, London
p18 Image © V&A Images / Victoria & Albert Museum, London
p19 Claire Roberts © 2010
p23 Copyright Dan Funderburgh
p24/25 Prints by Deanne Cheuk, clothing and photos by Sue Stemp
p27 Design by Studio Tord Boontje for Kvadrat
p28 Blue Floral-Spring Summer 2010 Collection, Paperchase Products Ltd.
p30 Courtesy of Catwalking.com
p32 Angel Chang
p37 Luisa Cevese Riedizioni
p39 Conserve HRP
p41 Design by Hella Jongerius for IKEA, 2009, photo by IKEA
p50 Lucy O'Brien

p61 Courtesy of Amsterstampa
p69 Claire Roberts © 2010
p70 Geoff McFetridge - Champion Graphics
p75 Green Ambush by Eno Henze for Exposif Wallpapers by Maxalot Gallery
p76 Surface2Air
p76 Alastair Wiper
p77 Courtesy of Catwalking.com
p82 Courtesy of Amsterstampa
p84 Alexandra Devaux (www.alexandradevaux.com)
p87 Copyright Adidas China, Style Essentials Spring/Summer 2009
p89 printpattern.blogspot.com 2011
p91 Courtesy of Amsterstampa
p92 Hannah Exall
p94 COLUMBIA/AMERICAN ZOETROPE/SONY / THE KOBAL COLLECTION
p95 Joasia Staszek
p96 Copyright Adidas China, Style Essentials Spring/Summer 2009
p97 Copyright Dan Funderburgh
p98 Claire Roberts © 2010
p101 Copyright Adidas China, Style Essentials Spring/Summer 2009
p106 Claire Roberts © 2010
p120 People Will Always need Plates
p121 Klaus Haapaniemi (Iittala)
p129 Image © V&A Images / Victoria & Albert Museum, London
p132 thomaspaul
p133 Abbey Watkins
p143 Alex Kohout
p150/151 Joasia Staszek
p154 Lucy O'Brien
p155 Lovefoxx, vocalist from Cansei de ser Sexy (CSS) for Design T-Shirts Store graniph: www.graniph.com
p158 Première Vision
p163 Courtesy of Amsterstampa
p168 Jason Thompson, Rag & Bone Bindery
p175 Design by Studio Tord Boontje for Kvadrat
P188 Fokus Fabrik
p190 Peter Ingwersen
p191 www.gossypium.co.uk copyright 2011 Gossypium

All other images © Alex Russell

Lynne Elvins/Naomi Goulder

Working with ethics

The Fundamentals
of Printed Textile
Design

Ethical:
aware-
ness/
reflect-
ion/
debate

Publisher's note

The subject of ethics is not new, yet its consideration within the applied visual arts is perhaps not as prevalent as it might be. Our aim here is to help a new generation of students, educators and practitioners find a methodology for structuring their thoughts and reflections in this vital area.

AVA Publishing hopes that these **Working with ethics** pages provide a platform for consideration and a flexible method for incorporating ethical concerns in the work of educators, students and professionals. Our approach consists of four parts:

The **introduction** is intended to be an accessible snapshot of the ethical landscape, both in terms of historical development and current dominant themes.

The **framework** positions ethical consideration into four areas and poses questions about the practical implications that might occur. Marking your response to each of these questions on the scale shown will allow your reactions to be further explored by comparison.

The **case study** sets out a real project and then poses some ethical questions for further consideration. This is a focus point for a debate rather than a critical analysis so there are no predetermined right or wrong answers.

A selection of **further reading** for you to consider areas of particular interest in more detail.

Introduction

Ethics is a complex subject that interlaces the idea of responsibilities to society with a wide range of considerations relevant to the character and happiness of the individual. It concerns virtues of compassion, loyalty and strength, but also of confidence, imagination, humour and optimism. As introduced in ancient Greek philosophy, the fundamental ethical question is: *what should I do*? How we might pursue a 'good' life not only raises moral concerns about the effects of our actions on others, but also personal concerns about our own integrity.

In modern times the most important and controversial questions in ethics have been the moral ones. With growing populations and improvements in mobility and communications, it is not surprising that considerations about how to structure our lives together on the planet should come to the forefront. For visual artists and communicators, it should be no surprise that these considerations will enter into the creative process.

Some ethical considerations are already enshrined in government laws and regulations or in professional codes of conduct. For example, plagiarism and breaches of confidentiality can be punishable offences. Legislation in various nations makes it unlawful to exclude people with disabilities from accessing information or spaces. The trade of ivory as a material has been banned in many countries. In these cases, a clear line has been drawn under what is unacceptable.

But most ethical matters remain open to debate, among experts and lay-people alike, and in the end we have to make our own choices on the basis of our own guiding principles or values. Is it more ethical to work for a charity than for a commercial company? Is it unethical to create something that others find ugly or offensive?

Specific questions such as these may lead to other questions that are more abstract. For example, is it only effects on humans (and what they care about) that are important, or might effects on the natural world require attention too?

Is promoting ethical consequences justified even when it requires ethical sacrifices along the way? Must there be a single unifying theory of ethics (such as the Utilitarian thesis that the right course of action is always the one that leads to the greatest happiness of the greatest number), or might there always be many different ethical values that pull a person in various directions?

As we enter into ethical debate and engage with these dilemmas on a personal and professional level, we may change our views or change our view of others. The real test though is whether, as we reflect on these matters, we change the way we act as well as the way we think. Socrates, the 'father' of philosophy, proposed that people will naturally do 'good' if they know what is right. But this point might only lead us to yet another question: *how do we know what is right?*

A framework for ethics

You
What are your ethical beliefs?

Central to everything you do will be your attitude to people and issues around you. For some people, their ethics are an active part of the decisions they make every day as a consumer, a voter or a working professional. Others may think about ethics very little and yet this does not automatically make them unethical. Personal beliefs, lifestyle, politics, nationality, religion, gender, class or education can all influence your ethical viewpoint.

Using the scale, where would you place yourself? What do you take into account to make your decision? Compare results with your friends or colleagues.

Your client
What are your terms?

Working relationships are central to whether ethics can be embedded into a project, and your conduct on a day-to-day basis is a demonstration of your professional ethics. The decision with the biggest impact is whom you choose to work with in the first place. Cigarette companies or arms traders are often-cited examples when talking about where a line might be drawn, but rarely are real situations so extreme. At what point might you turn down a project on ethical grounds and how much does the reality of having to earn a living affect your ability to choose?

Using the scale, where would you place a project? How does this compare to your personal ethical level?

01 02 03 04 05 06 07 08 09 10

01 02 03 04 05 06 07 08 09 10

Your specifications

What are the impacts of your materials?

In relatively recent times, we are learning that many natural materials are in short supply. At the same time, we are increasingly aware that some man-made materials can have harmful, long-term effects on people or the planet. How much do you know about the materials that you use? Do you know where they come from, how far they travel and under what conditions they are obtained? When your creation is no longer needed, will it be easy and safe to recycle? Will it disappear without a trace? Are these considerations your responsibility or are they out of your hands?

Using the scale, mark how ethical your material choices are.

Your creation

What is the purpose of your work?

Between you, your colleagues and an agreed brief, what will your creation achieve? What purpose will it have in society and will it make a positive contribution? Should your work result in more than commercial success or industry awards? Might your creation help save lives, educate, protect or inspire? Form and function are two established aspects of judging a creation, but there is little consensus on the obligations of visual artists and communicators toward society, or the role they might have in solving social or environmental problems. If you want recognition for being the creator, how responsible are you for what you create and where might that responsibility end?

Using the scale, mark how ethical the purpose of your work is.

01 02 03 04 05 06 07 08 09 10

01 02 03 04 05 06 07 08 09 10

One aspect of textile design that raises an ethical dilemma is in preserving the cultural traditions of small communities. Woven or handcrafted fabrics and garments can become valuable and highly prized purchases for wealthy collectors, tourists or museums. But this may not provide the community with the continuous flow of income necessary to sustain its needs. Old traditions and styles are being exchanged for more efficient, modern techniques. Commercial pressure to focus on simple designs that are easier to produce in quantity rather than quality pieces that require creativity and complexity is increasingly common. Young people are moving away from small communities and so the knowledge is no longer passed down from generation to generation. How much responsibility should a textile designer take if they want to draw inspiration from traditional designs or techniques? Even if designers wish to prevent the disappearance of traditional methods, what might they most usefully do?

Denim was produced as early as the sixteenth century using a twill weave with un-dyed weft yarn and coloured warp, which created the distinctive diagonal ribbing in the fabric. It was worn by workers because of its strength and durability. The term 'jeans' is said to originate from *Bleu de Genes*, meaning blue material from Genoa, Italy. Baggy denim became the uniform of choice for Genoese sailors and fishermen.

Synonymous with denim, indigo dye has become one of the most important commercial colourants because of the demand for jeans. It was originally derived from plants that were known for their ability to colour fabrics a deep blue. But the natural extraction process was expensive and could not produce the mass quantities required for the expanding market. In 1883, Adolf von Baeyer researched indigo's chemical structure and produced the first commercial production of the synthetic dye for which he received the Nobel Prize in 1905. In more recent years, the synthetic-dye industry has increased environmental standards to reduce the impacts of toxic waste from dye processes. However, there are still companies that flout regulations.

As the world's most popular fibre, cotton farming accounts for around ten per cent of worldwide pesticide use. Although the market for organic pesticide-free cotton is growing, it still represents less than one per cent of global trade. Cotton production also consumes huge quantities of water. In 2007, the Levi Strauss company began assessing the environmental impacts of their 501 jeans and found that more than 3,000 litres of water were used during the complete product cycle. Of this, 49 per cent was used to grow the cotton, 45 per cent is used when people wash their jeans at home and the remaining six per cent is used during the manufacturing process. As a result of their findings, the company is now working on a 'Water<Less' jeans project.

According to Mintel, in 2007, three pairs of jeans were sold every second of every day in Great Britain; with imports totaling approximately 86 million pairs. In a global survey, more than six out of ten people said they love or enjoy wearing denim.

Does the global expansion of a market always represent success?

Is it more ethical to use natural rather than synthetic dyes?

Would you buy a pair of fair trade cotton and organic jeans from an alternative brand, one which has certified ethical standards as an essential part of their operations, as opposed to a market-leading brand?

I wish I had invented blue jeans. They have expression, modesty, sex appeal, simplicity – all I hope for in my clothes.

Yves Saint Laurent

Further reading

AIGA
Design Business and Ethics
2007, AIGA

Eaton, Marcia Muelder
Aesthetics and the Good Life
1989, Associated University Press

Ellison, David
Ethics and Aesthetics in European Modernist Literature:
From the Sublime to the Uncanny
2001, Cambridge University Press

Fenner, David E W (Ed)
Ethics and the Arts:
An Anthology
1995, Garland Reference Library of Social Science

Gini, Al and Marcoux, Alexei M
Case Studies in Business Ethics
2005, Prentice Hall

McDonough, William and Braungart, Michael
Cradle to Cradle:
Remaking the Way We Make Things
2002, North Point Press

Papanek, Victor
Design for the Real World:
Making to Measure
1972, Thames & Hudson

United Nations Global Compact
The Ten Principles
www.unglobalcompact.org/AboutTheGC/TheTenPrinciples/index.
html